Acceptance and Mindfulness Toolbox

For Children & Adolescents

75+ Worksheets & Activities for
Trauma, Anxiety, Depression, Anger & More

Timothy Gordon, MSW • Jessica Borushok, PhD

Published by
PESI Publishing & Media
PESI, Inc
3839 White Ave
Eau Claire, WI 54703

Cover: Amy Rubenzer
Editing: Bookmasters
Layout: Amy Rubenzer & Bookmasters

ISBN: 9781683732235

Printed in the United States of America.

PESI
Publishing
& Media
pesipublishing.com

About the Authors

Timothy Gordon, MSW, is a social worker in Canada and an internationally recognized, peer-reviewed Acceptance and Commitment Therapy (ACT) trainer. He specializes in treating attachment and trauma-related disorders, and is passionate about making therapy practical and engaging for the young people he works with through art, play, and experiential exercises. Tim is also a yoga teacher who integrates movement and yoga practices into his work. His research has included yoga as a mental health intervention, ACT for chronic pain, ACT with neonatal intensive care units, as well as acceptance and mindfulness with Canada's Parliament. Visit Tim's website: www.thezensocialworker.ca

Jessica Borushok, PhD, is a clinical psychologist and founder of Busy Mind Reboot. She has consulted on a multi-site, grant-funded program to help parents of children in neonatal intensive care units and has co-facilitated a classroom-based prevention program for fourth graders designed to teach problem solving and coping skills in an effort to reduce risk associated with environmental stressors. In addition to clinical work and research, Dr. Borushok provides ACT trainings. Visit Jessica's website: www.busymindreboot.com

Dedication

For Quinn
- Timothy Gordon

For my family and friends.
I am forever grateful.
- Jessica Borushok

Table of Contents

Introduction

Acceptance and mindfulness approaches have gained widespread interest with application to almost every population you can imagine from test-taking anxiety to even severe health concerns. Many different theoretical orientations and styles of practice have made this possible.

Our goal for this book is to bring the practical, evidence-based tools of Acceptance and Commitment Therapy (ACT), attachment science, Dialectical Behavior Therapy (DBT), Mindfulness-Based Stress Reduction (MBSR), Mindfulness-Based Cognitive Therapy (MBCT), and yoga to the great work you are already doing in the form of worksheets, exercises, games, mindfulness scripts, and so much more. Each of these frameworks provide insights into appropriate treatment of children and adolescents who face difficulties. **We have found a common ground unifying all of these approaches in a single, transdiagnostic model: They encourage experiential activities, where a client comes in direct contact with the processes of change being used in the clinician's office, classroom, or practice setting.**

This workbook is your proverbial toolbox in using the processes of acceptance, mindfulness, values, and commitment to change behavior in creative and engaging ways. We have presented you with a collection of our favorite exercises and worksheets that we have found useful in the work we do. **We have used every page of what we're sharing in this toolbox with children, adolescents, and caregivers—educating them and offering skill building.**

As a brief overview, this book specifically targets the following clinical problems:

- Attachment and relational issues
- Anger and hostile behavior
- Antisocial behavior
- Anxiety, stress, and worry
- Bullying
- Depression and sadness
- Eating-disordered behavior
- Gender and sexual identity concerns
- Life changes and transitions
- Obsessive-compulsive disorder and trichotillomania
- School refusal
- Self-harm and suicidal ideation
- Substance abuse and impulsivity
- Trauma and trauma-related problems

How to Use This Book

This book is filled with exercises, worksheets, and activities to use with children, adolescents, and their caregivers that make up the best of the work we do, and yet we would be remiss if we provided you with these excellent materials without any context to use them. The first section of this book takes a brief dive into the science, theory, and philosophy that underpins all the great skills we use. We promise that it only includes the information you need to know and is in no way exhaustive.

Rather, we pose a fun challenge to you in this first section: Apply the science informing our unified approach to any client or clinical situation you may find yourself in. This section will allow you to apply and adapt the worksheets, exercises, and activities in this book to the specific populations with whom you work and settings in which you work.

Whether you find yourself working with an anxious 5-year-old who is struggling with separation from caregivers and refuses to go to school, or a depressed 13-year-old transgender youth who is self-harming—having hormone treatments withheld by the medical system and has threatened suicide—the processes are the same, and your clinical decision of what is developmentally appropriate for this youth will guide what you do next.

The rest of this book focuses on how to implement these practices: What are the exercises and worksheets you can use to encourage acceptance and mindfulness in the youth you work with, and build flexibility in the people who care for them?

This book follows the structure of treatment. We begin with tools designed to assess, conceptualize, and set a context for change using acceptance and mindfulness practices. Then, we lay out a plethora of treatment and skill-building resources for you to use in sessions with your clients, with modifications based on developmental levels and considerations for different age groups.

We wrap up the book with insights and skills on how to generalize the work completed in session to other contexts in your client's life: at home, school, or in other interpersonal interactions. We do this, in part, through providing plans and strategies for interacting with and training caregivers so that they can reinforce and expand on the work we do in session at home and in school.

We are so excited to share this fun, practical guide with you and can't wait to see how you take these skills and adopt them into your work for fostering acceptance and mindfulness in your clients.

Having Fun with Science

A cceptance and mindfulness has a certain vibe. It can evoke images of meditation cushions, yoga postures, Eastern spirituality, and philosophical discussions about the inevitability of pain in life and the true wisdom of the universe. We like these images and yet also recognize that acceptance and mindfulness practices come with a rich background in science to support them.

Our reasoning behind spending a little time explaining the science of acceptance and mindfulness—besides the fact that we're giant nerds—is that an understanding in basic science allows you to be more flexible and more creative with the tools we will provide. If you understand the foundation of this work, then you can begin to adapt, think critically about, or more spontaneously introduce these skills.

WHY ACCEPTANCE AND MINDFULNESS?

This work is easy to understand and apply immediately. To get started, you need to understand a few basic concepts. We elect to use acceptance or a willingness to be open, come into contact with, and be receptive to difficult experiences as our approach rather than a control or symptom-reduction agenda that attempts to challenge, dispute, distract, or argue with painful content, such as thoughts, feelings, memories, and physical sensations.

This approach is based on an unexpected scientific development that is the underpinning of modern approaches to Cognitive Behavioral Therapy: namely, Acceptance and Commitment Therapy (ACT), Compassion Focused Therapy (CFT), Dialectical Behavior Therapy (DBT), Functional Analytic Psychotherapy (FAP), and Mindfulness-Based Cognitive Therapy (MBCT), which are the most prevalent, but there are many other examples. This scientific development highlights that, contrary to popular assumptions, we cannot erase, delete, or otherwise permanently remove painful lived experiences such as thoughts. We can, however, create new relationships to our pain so that it doesn't overwhelm us or dictate our lives. It also means that instead of focusing on whether something is true or false, right or wrong, good or bad, we look at how a certain behavior or experience is working (functions) in a given moment (context). That's where mindfulness comes in!

Through helping young people notice, describe, be curious about, and otherwise engage with their full experience in the present moment, they are better able to see which behaviors work and which don't. A young girl who hits when she feels angry can realize that hitting may feel good in the moment, but then it only makes the situation worse as she gets in trouble. If we can teach her to notice early signs that she is feeling angry and slow down that process, then we can begin to train her to try out different behaviors when anger shows up that may work better for her in the long run.

> **Our goal is to help young folks and their caregivers get better at noticing their experience and the function of their behaviors (i.e., why they do what they do), sitting with their pain, and choosing alternative behaviors that work better for everyone involved.**

FOCUS ON WHAT YOUNG PEOPLE DO!

Paying attention to what happens as a result of what young people do (the consequences of their behavior) might seem obvious at first, but we assure you, it's more common to reach for a complicated explanation that gets stuck in the content of what is happening rather than the context. Understanding what the young people you're working with do and focusing on what happens as a result assists you in understanding why they keep doing what they do. That teen who threatens suicide, what happens when they do that? If you don't know, ask!

For example, when working with a teenage girl who frequently threatened suicide, we noticed that she received a lot of attention from, and time with, her mother after texting a suicide note. Using this acceptance-based approach, we were able to present this young woman with our analysis of how her behavior works in that situation. We explored her history of attachment disruption, specifically her experience of not getting her emotional needs met. She became comfortable talking about suicidal ideation and explained that in the moment that she threatened suicide, she didn't have any other words to say, "I need you, what I feel is unbearable." When we all identified the function of her behavior to threaten suicide, we were able to work on trying new ways to get her emotional needs met and communicate in these painful situations.

Here's another example that might not seem so obvious. When working with a 5-year-old boy who presented as being extremely anxious about his parents leaving the home and would refuse to go to school, the reinforcing nature of his behavior was not obvious to either of us in looking at this young boy who was clearly suffering. It wasn't until we began to understand that his **attempts** to control his fears and phobias were highly reinforcing *in the moment*.

This is important because the external, observable consequences of his behavior (getting in trouble with his parents) did not appear to be reinforcing at all, but when we analyzed the function of his behavior and interviewed him explicitly about attempting to block his parents' departure from the home and refusing to attend school, we found that his anxiety and fear was so overwhelming that to do *anything* to control or avoid a feared outcome felt like the "right" thing in the moment. He knew he couldn't actually stop his parents from leaving, but he was so fearful of what could happen that even attempting to stop them provided some relief—at least he was doing something! With some distance from those sticky situations, he could identify that it made things worse to fight with his parents. Through working on distress tolerance, acceptance, and commitment to behavior change, he could develop new responses to anxiety and fear.

UNDERSTAND WHAT MAKES EXPERIENCES HARD

The work that you do using this acceptance and mindfulness approach will focus on the thoughts, feelings, sensations, and memories that make life difficult for your young clients. When you think of a child who is refusing to go to school, it's relevant at times to focus on environmental factors, such as a bully, and advocating for a systemic intervention. However, the bulk of this book invites a closer look at the internal, private world of a young person. This isn't to say the environmental factors are inconsequential. They're important and necessary to understand. Rather, we want to highlight that acceptance and mindfulness is about working with painful private content (thoughts, feelings, sensations, and memories) young clients experience and recognizing that they may likely attempt to avoid, control, or escape this painful private content by manipulating what they can: whether they go to school or not, arguing or yelling, hiding, etc.

When a young person takes a thought as literal or is really stuck on some private experience (a thought, feeling, sensation, or memory) and we observe that content governing his or her behavior, perhaps causing a problematic outcome, we call this fusion. For example, the young boy mentioned previously may be having terrifying thoughts that something bad will happen to his parents if they leave. Since he buys into or believes these thoughts to be true, he is trying everything he can to stop his parents from leaving even if it's causing additional problems.

The problem is not the terrifying thought. The problem is that when he believes this thought, his response to it causes problems in his life. The term **fusion** is important because we can get fused with all kinds of stuff. And it's helpful to remember that fusion is not necessarily always bad. When you're watching a great movie, you want to suspend disbelief and be really fused with what's happening in the scene; you want to feel that the characters and story are real. This fusion helps you enjoy the film. Alternatively, if you're overly fused with the scary scene that happened in the movie, all of a sudden you may begin to assume every creak or tiny noise in your home is a threat and do something out of character. It's all about the context and function. Does getting sucked into that thought, feeling, memory, or physical sensation help?

For most of our young clients, we'd argue that the reason they are coming to therapy (or their caregivers are making them come) is because their strategies for coping with difficult experiences are problematic—they are not working. In this acceptance and mindfulness approach, rather than directly challenging, disputing, or generally trying to cognitively restructure fused content, we instead promote **flexibility**.

> **Being psychologically flexible simply means we bring young people in contact with their painful content to learn to do new things in the presence of it.**

USE VALUES TO TARGET LONG-TERM BEHAVIOR CHANGE

To effect change in behavior positively, we need to know who and what is reinforcing to a young client. We've come up with a fun phrase to use in session with caregivers: "Your attention is the watering can of life: The behaviors you pay attention to are the ones you will see grow." What we mean here is that even a caregiver's attention—looking at a young person, noticing them and their behavior—can be reinforcing. Early on in treatment, it can be helpful to see whose attention is reinforcing to a young client. In working with adolescents, caregivers may find that their attention is not as reinforcing than, say, their peer group, and this can make establishing exactly what is reinforcing to an adolescent more complicated.

Furthermore, we get bigger feats of behavior change with young people by learning who and what is most important to them. We use that information to evoke a focus on new behavior that grows their lives in a meaningful way, rather than focusing on reducing symptoms.

Also, let's just be frank for a moment: Young people tend to be very practical and outcome focused. In our experience, young people need an explanation of *why* they would choose to do this work with you, and that is what a commitment to values-driven behavior is about: coming in contact with painful stuff so that they can live bigger, juicier, better lives! And of course, bigger, juicier, better lives is about what is uniquely important to each of them. This commitment to values-driven behavior is how we target an increase in long-term quality of life.

Now on to the fun stuff!

Beginning and Assessment

This chapter will guide you through beginning your work with a young person. We have included worksheets and games for initiating the first meeting and facilitating both learning about the young person you're working with, including their interests, as well as establishing a therapeutic contract with an informed consent to help your young client understand what your work will entail. We have included some assessment activities, but most importantly, we begin the chapter with something special in this acceptance and mindfulness approach: priming the therapeutic alliance with values.

STARTING WITH VALUES
PRIMING THE ALLIANCE WITH VALUES

Many interpretations exist for how you might begin your work with young people. In some practice settings, structured intake sessions are a must, or formal assessment measures may be required. Do what is required of you by your practice context and licensing regulatory body, and at the earliest feasible opportunity, ask your clients to tell you about their values, who and what is most important to them. We do this to prime our clients to focus on the life they want to live and what is most important to them, rather than focusing on deficits, pathology, and problems. This helps set the stage for treatment goals that focus on growth.

We seek to make therapy the type of environment that is friendly and fun at times, so that we may address difficult topics with ease rather than therapy being an aversive environment where we only talk about painful things. We cannot underscore this enough: In our experience, clients, and especially caregivers, come to therapy wanting to fix young people or make things instantly better. This early focus on values interrupts that conventional agenda and is an example of stimulus control where the therapist hopes to create a practice setting where clients come to build on strengths, improve behavior, and reinforce the behaviors they wish to maintain rather than self-stigmatize or complain. **We will show you examples of how to work within the parameters of your setting to create a context for change, while respecting and following the guidelines and practices of your setting or profession.**

In the following ad lib worksheet, What's Important About Me, we encourage young people to share with us information that may not seem pertinent about the problem they are presenting with. Of course, the information in this ad lib activity is incredibly valuable in our analysis of who they are, what's important to them, and what they want their life to be about. We have also had a lot of success doing this worksheet with primary caregivers and the young people they present with in session together. The What's Important About Us worksheet provides an adaptation that a caregiver and young person can do together in session.

The caregiver worksheet is an early attempt at creating a non-eliminative therapeutic contract in favor of an acceptance-based contract that instead focuses on values, highlighting what is important and what is hoped for in the future. We've noticed that this activity evokes a lot of laughter and sets the right tone for beginning therapeutic work with families that undermines the "fix my kid" agenda.

What's Important About Me

My name is _____ and some important things to know about me are that my favorite color is _____ and my favorite food is _____.

My favorite thing to do is _____.

A part of why I like to do that is because it's _____.

Something I'm really good at is _____.

What you should know about me is that being here makes me feel _____

_____.

And I'm hopeful that from therapy we will _____.

How you know I'm doing okay is when I _____ or say _____.

If I'm not doing okay, I might _____ or say _____.

In therapy, it's important to me that we work on _____

and talk about _____.

Something that's going to make it hard to talk about this is feeling

_____.

What's Important About Us

My favorite thing about _____ is their _____.

It stands out to me especially when they _____.

I enjoy this about them because _____.

They're really good at _____.

And I appreciate this because _____.

What's important to know about them is that they _____.

I know that they struggle with _____.

My hope for them in the future is that they will be _____.

This is important to me because _____.

I especially like it when they _____.

My favorite thing to do with them is _____.

I hope that one day they will _____.

What I hope they see in me is that I'm _____.

Something I think we should talk about in therapy is _____.

I wish that one day, together, we will _____.

Choosing Values

Some young people have strong opinions about who and what is most important to them, and others do not. Let's face it, having a strong connection to your values and actually knowing explicitly what they are can be complicated work for adults—let alone young people! We've made a list of values that the young people you work with might care about. Don't hesitate to be creative, adding to our list or making your own.

We recommend you make a copy of the list below and invite the young person you work with to pick out the five values that are the most meaningful to them.

Acceptance to Listen to Others

Accepting Myself

Accepting Others

Achievement in Accomplishing What Matters

Adventure

Appreciating the Small Things

Being a Visionary, Changing the World

Being Appreciated

Being Artistic

Being Caring to Treat Everything Around Me with Tenderness and Love

Being Creative and Inventive: To Have Ideas and Use Them

Being Creative to Express Myself

Being Emotional to Share How I Feel

Being Free to Do What I Choose

Being Friendly

Being Healthy to Nurture Myself

Being Helpful in Doing Good Things for Others

Being Myself

Being Responsible

Being Social to Enjoy Listening and Talking to Others

Being Thankful for What I Have in My Life

Courage to Take Action Even When I Feel Fear

Curiosity to Explore New Experiences

Education and Learning

Encouraging the Potential in Everyone

Excitement to Chase New Things in Life

Exploration to Try New Things

Feeling Good

Feeling Like I Belong

Feeling Safe

Flexibility to Handle Change

Forgiveness

Generosity to Share My Unique Gifts and Talents

Giving Compassion to Show Others They are Loved

Giving Love and Being Loved

Giving Thanks

Growth in Finding Opportunities to Learn

Happiness to Smile, Laugh, and Enjoy Life

Having a Connection with People

Having Quality Time

Helping Others

Honesty and Telling the Truth

Leadership to Create What I Want in the World

Nature and the Outdoors

Peacefulness

Physical Activity

Playfulness to Have Fun

Positivity

Pride to Feel Good About Who I Am and What I Do

Self-Compassion to Take Care of My Mind, Body, and Spirit

Self-Reflection to Look Inside Myself

Spirituality or Religion

The Environment, Caring for the World

Trusting and Being Trusted

Understanding Others

Wisdom to Find Answers within Myself

Then, transfer these values onto cards that you can print and cut out for the client. Here is an example of how you may print out the cards.

Giving Love & Being Loved

Spirituality or Religion

Being Responsible

Helping Others

Education & Learning

Nature & the Outdoors

Your Inner Strength

In the next worksheet, clients draw or write in their strengths in the outline of a person. This exercise highlights that these strengths are private experiences and also helps clients notice where they experience these strengths in their body. For example, a client might write *kind* over their heart, *smart* in their head, or *funny* in their belly.

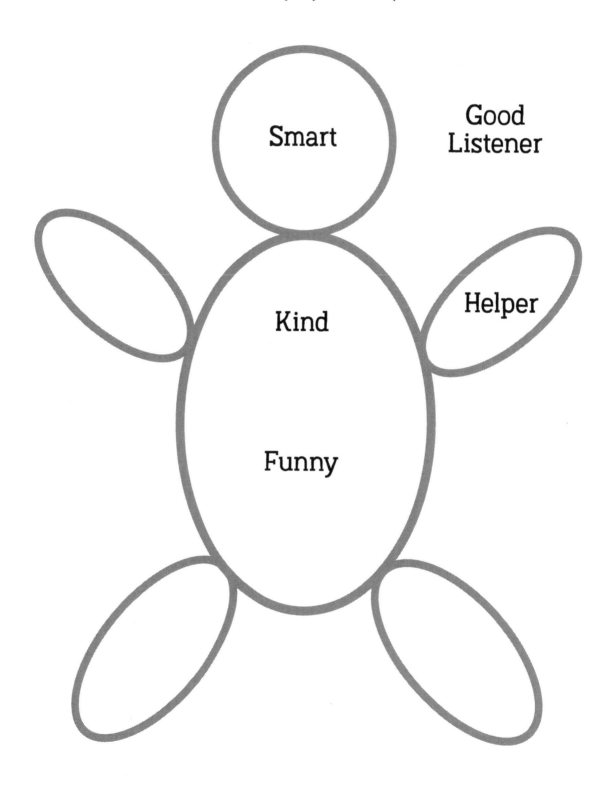

Your Inner Strength

Sometimes being strong doesn't mean that you just have big muscles, it also means that you can identify what's special about you. Write the things that show how strong you are on the inside (smart, kind, funny, creative, good listener, helper) and where they go inside you.

What I Want to Be About

In this art activity, we encourage the young people we work with to depict abstractly or literally the qualities they would like to have by identifying different people, animals, or creatures (real, fictional, or imagined) that represent these qualities. We have heard answers as varied as *super*, like being a superhero, or *calm*, like a caregiver of theirs.

What I Want to Be About

Which people, animals, or creatures (real, fictional or imagined) have qualities or characteristics that you like? Draw them below and write down how you want to be more like them.

How I can be more

like _____.

How I can be more

like _____.

LEARNING ABOUT WHAT HURTS

My Origin Story

This worksheet is appropriate for older children and adolescents. We usually preface this worksheet by saying, "Every superhero has an origin story, an explanation of where they came from that helps us understand why they do what they do. Sometimes, those origin stories are scary, sad, or both—like when Bruce Wayne, who later became Batman, witnessed his parents' murder. We're going to make a small comic about your origin story."

In this worksheet, we give you several panes of a comic book. The goal is for the client to draw and write dialogue for their origin story: what happened/when, how it was difficult, the strengths that were uncovered, and what this means today.

My Origin Story

Every hero has a journey of overcoming their past to become something even greater. Draw out yours: What happened/when, how it was difficult, the strengths that were uncovered, and what this means today.

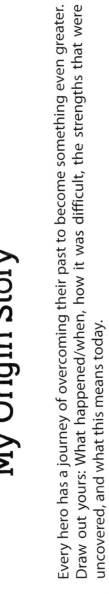

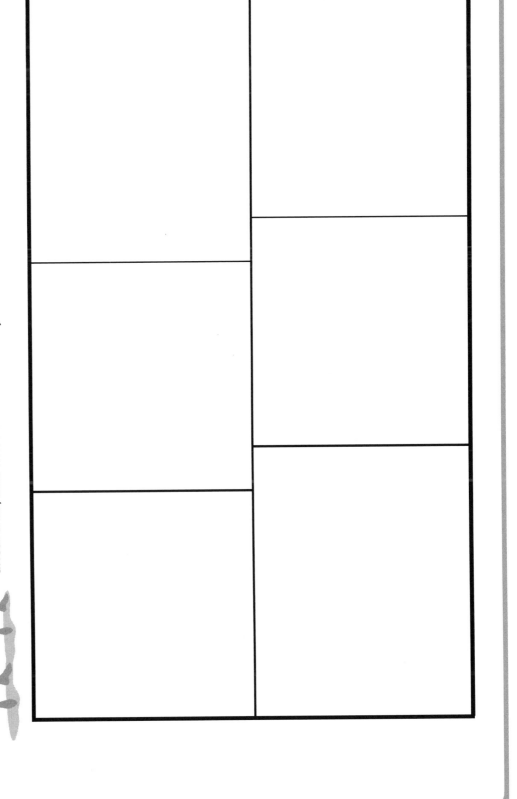

Who's Your Monster?

In this art activity, we facilitate a conversation focused on painful thoughts, feelings, sensations, and memories that are depicted as a yucky feelings monster. We want to know what painful stuff shows up for the client. It can sometimes be easy to fall into the habit of judging young clients' experiences as being negative or bad. Remember, they're simply difficult for the young person, not something inherently wrong. We seek to expose those difficulties—identifying what they are and changing the young person's relationship to them—by looking at those experiences in a new way.

Before beginning any drawing, explain that the purpose of the activity is to talk about and depict the difficult stuff inside so that we can more easily work with it. We find that being practical is a useful way in proceeding, and we say, "Drawing and talking about our difficulties can help us both. It helps me to better understand what you're struggling with, and it can help you by identifying and labeling it."

Materials

- Art supplies: You can simply use a piece of paper and colored pencils or markers, but we'd like to encourage you to use stencils and other supplies to assist the young person you're working with in making their depiction more elaborate.

Prompts for Depicting Your Client's Yucky Feelings Monster

- "Think about the difficult thoughts, feelings, memories, or sensations that you struggle with. Try to be specific."

Clinician Note

If the client is having difficulty thinking of things, use examples you're aware of in this young person's life—i.e., sadness, fear, worry, or difficult situations you know they struggle with—and identify what they feel in those situations.

- "Imagine that these yucky feelings you struggle with could take the form of a monster. Really picture it. How big would it be? What color is it? Does it have claws or wings? Does it breathe fire? How big is it in comparison to you?"

- "Using any of the art materials you choose, depict your yucky feelings monster."

Just as important as the art activity is, so is the debriefing activity after they have drawn their yucky feelings monster and themselves. Take time to explore the details of what your client depicted, being curious about what they chose to depict and didn't. There's no need to infer too much about their depiction, there's a lot of utility in training a conversational mindfulness where the young person you're working with identifies their own thoughts, feelings, sensations, and memories that they might typically avoid. This art activity offers a different kind of interaction with the pain that makes up their monster.

Trapped By Your Inner Bully

On the following worksheet, ask a young client to draw what they do when they feel trapped by their inner bullies. This is a way for clients to identify the behaviors they do (and their consequences) when they listen to their inner bullies (private experiences).

Trapped by
Your Inner Bully

Sometimes our inner bullies trap us and keep us from what is important. What do you do when you're trapped? Maybe you hit, make fun of someone, stay at home, yell, steal, hide, don't raise your hand in class, sit by yourself. In each of the boxes, write down one way you react when you feel trapped; then draw a picture in the space below of what this looks like to you.

What's Not Working?

This next worksheet is a great exercise to do in session with young people. We have effectively implemented this worksheet with children as young as seven, with adolescents, and with families.

Although we're providing you with a worksheet, you can also adapt this as an exercise in session using a whiteboard, blackboard, or oversized piece of paper if that is available to you, and then send the client home with the worksheet to practice with experiences that pop up over the week.

This exercise specifically seeks to demonstrate the immediate reinforcing qualities of attempting to escape, control, or avoid painful experiences, as well as the long-term workability and impact of these attempts. To be explicit, this exercise trains young people (and perhaps their caregivers) to do a functional analysis.

What's Not Working?
Taking a Closer Look at the Things We Do When Pain Shows Up

How This Works

On the right you will write down painful experiences you have and what you do when those painful experiences show up. Then you will follow the instructions below and score how well those strategies are working.

Scoring Our Strategies

Go through each of your doing and thinking strategies and score whether it helps you avoid or escape pain in the short term, permanently deletes your pain so it never returns, and/or helps you move closer to your values (the people and things in your life that matter to you) in the long term.

Scoring Symbols

Use the symbols below to score each strategy.

 Helps me escape or avoid my painful experiences for a little while.

 Helps me permanently delete my painful experiences so they never return.

 Helps me move closer to my values in the long term.

Painful Experiences

Painful Thoughts   Painful Sensations

Painful Feelings   Painful Memories

What I Do When Pain Shows Up

Doing Strategies (How I Behave)

Thinking Strategies (such as worrying, thinking of the worst outcome, thinking about situation over and over again)

Know Your Hooks

A hook is anything that impacts your behavior. Once you bite that hook, it reels you in and you no longer get to choose what happens next. For most people, hooks (such as painful thoughts, feelings, memories, or physical sensations) are so out of our awareness that we begin to engage in problematic behaviors before we are even aware of this.

This worksheet can help your young clients begin to identify their hooks, the common behaviors they engage in as a response to their hooks, and what they would like to do instead when hooks show up.

This worksheet even offers an opportunity to label or identify what the hook is (anger hook, lonely hook) so that they are better prepared to identify the hook in the future. The goal is to help young people notice their hooks before they bite them so that they are in control of what happens next. There is also a hooks-tracking worksheet to help young clients track multiple hooks that happen over the course of a week.

Know Your Hooks

A hook is any experience that impacts your behavior.
Once you bite it, it reels you in and decides what happens next.

1. What Happened?

Write down a situation where you did something problematic, or something you wish you had done differently. What did you do?

2. Pay Attention

Write down what thoughts, feelings, memories, or physical sensations showed up for you that led to the problematic behavior.

3. Is That a Hook?

Ask yourself if that private experience is a hook for you. Here's how you can tell: Did that thought, feeling, memory, or physical sensation cause you to act in a way you didn't want to? If so, give that hook a name to help identify it (i.e., my anxiety hook, "I'm unloveable" hook, etc.).

4. Prepare

The next time that hook shows up, what do you want to do instead?

Notice Your Hooks

Noticing your hooks can help you in many ways. You don't get to choose whether you have hooks or not but you can choose what you do when they show up. Take time over the next week to intentionally pay attention to when hooks show up. They can be sneaky sometimes.

Daily Hook Tracker

When & Where	Hook	Response To Hook

FOUNDATIONAL SKILLS TRAINING

Thoughts, Feelings, Sensations, Memories

Identifying specific private experiences is made fun with this worksheet that can be turned into an exercise in session. We divide experiences into four different categories:

- **Thoughts:** the things we think
- **Feelings:** emotions that occur to us
- **Memories:** past situations and recollections
- **Sensations:** the physical perception of what comes in contact with the body including touch, smell, sight, sound, and taste

You can easily turn the worksheet into an exercise in session by inviting the young people you work with to keep track of thoughts, feelings, memories, and sensations that they're noticing with you.

Regardless of whether you do an exercise in session or not, we highly recommend sending young people home with this worksheet so that they can repeat the activity of tracking different experiences. Remember, we're training them to be mindful of what they notice, and we wish to do this in a non-evocative way at first, so you might assign them a task such as, "On your way home today, keep track of the different experiences you notice. We're learning how to pay attention to what's happening in our world."

The worksheet offers four different opportunities to track private (inside) experiences of thoughts, feelings, memories, and sensations represented with a thought bubble (for thoughts), heart (for feelings), picture frame (for memories), and hand (for sensations).

Thoughts, Feelings, Sensations, Memories

Experience: _____

_____

Experience: _____

_____

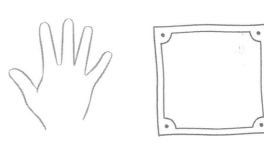

Experience: _____

_____

Experience: _____

_____

Response or Reaction?

Showing young people how acceptance and mindfulness can work is arguably essential to this approach—it can also be a lot of fun! Giving practical demonstrations are a big part of our approach in bringing the processes of acceptance and mindfulness alive in a session.

Take, for example, a young girl we worked with who was refusing to attend school. We did this exercise as an early way to socialize her to how her mind works, training her to recognize that there is a difference between reacting to something spontaneously versus noticing an experience and choosing how to respond. The young girl we worked with was able to use this exercise to help us understand what made going to school so difficult—that there were difficult thoughts and feelings that came up in reaction to attending school in the morning.

This exercise made those experiences more explicit, which in turn allowed us to use specific activities from this book (such as "Who's Your Monster?") to help her pay more attention to the difficult feelings and later targeting her reaction to those difficulties with a graded approach to returning to school. The most exciting part about this early intervention is that it worked—we were able to get her buy-in and show her that we could validate what was difficult for her about attending school while simultaneously offering a path forward.

Instructions

- Describe the purpose of this activity, which is noticing the difference between reacting to something and choosing how to handle a situation.

- Pick a lightweight object, such as a pen, crumpled-up paper, or a tissue box to throw.

- Explain to your client that this exercise involves physical engagement that might take them off guard momentarily, and get their consent for this activity. We often tell the young person we work with, "I'm going to throw this tissue box at you in a moment, and I want you to notice what you do in reaction."

- Gently throw the lightweight object, observing what your young client does, then asking them, "What happened?"

- Most young people we work with will catch the object we throw. Regardless of what they do (catch or otherwise), point out that they did *something*.

- Pause for a moment and ask your client if they *chose* what they did, or if it was a reaction.

Clinician Note

You may need to explain what a reaction is. Our favorite way of describing a reaction is using the example of falling: You don't have to think to put your hands out and brace yourself; it just happens almost automatically. Alternatively, we'll also have young people stand up straight and fall forward, pointing out that one leg will kick forward to balance. This is what we mean by reaction: a behavior that lacks forethought.

- Repeat the activity, this time encouraging your client to choose a different way of handling the lightweight object being thrown at them.

- Once again, inquire if they *chose* how they responded this time as the lightweight object was coming towards them. On occasion, we will get a genuine reaction from the young person we're working with—perhaps they're taken off-guard by the sudden physical movement necessitating another repeat. Other times, we will repeat this portion of explicit choice with the young person for the sake of making our point salient.

- Discuss the difference between reacting and responding. Ask your client to describe how reacting and responding are different.

- Conclude the exercise by inviting your client to imagine a situation they have struggled with in their life where they have reacted. Ask them what they notice when applying this new way of thinking to that difficult situation. We have had a lot of success by asking simply: "What about that situation has you reacting?"

A word of caution in debriefing this exercise: Be careful not to dichotomize reacting and responding, presenting reactions as bad or unworkable. We find it helpful to describe reactions as necessary—for example, when touching a hot surface that could burn bare skin, such as a stove, the immediate reaction to recoil is helpful.

In debriefing this exercise, note the felt difference between reacting and responding, specifically how the young person you're working with experiences each. If your young client has difficulty describing or cannot tell you what makes a specific situation difficult and reactive for them, encourage them to pay attention the next time they encounter the situation, directing them to intentionally track how the experience impacts them. The situation might also be workable for doing an exposure session where you take the time to specifically draw your young client's attention to their reactions in contrast to perceived choices.

Feelings Tic-Tac-Toe

We have created this game, which first appeared in *The ACT Approach* (2017), inspired by McHugh, Bobarnac, and Reed's (2011) research on teaching situation-based emotions. This game involves therapist participation—both the young person and you will play!

Draw a tic-tac-toe board on a whiteboard or piece of paper with two vertical lines and two intersecting horizontal lines spaced at least an inch apart—but larger can be more fun if the space is available. The game board has nine spaces where typically players draw X's and O's to achieve three in a row. Instead of drawing X's and O's, instruct your clients to draw a feeling face.

Beginning this game by drawing your own examples of feeling faces is best. In the following example, we've depicted:

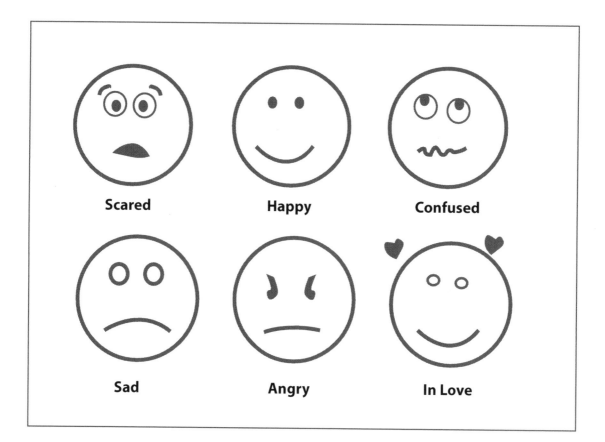

Scared   Happy   Confused

Sad   Angry   In Love

The following are more feeling faces for additional variation in your feelings tic-tac-toe games:

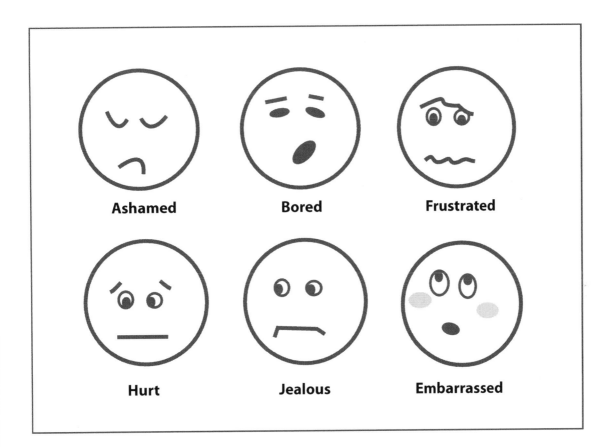

In the game, you and the young client take turns drawing feeling faces. Similar to tic-tac-toe, the first person to draw three different feeling faces in a row wins. Unlike tic-tac-toe, when you draw a feeling face you then have to describe a time when you felt that way. When it is your turn, we recommend that you use examples the young person may relate to. This is a helpful way to get clients comfortable talking about feelings and experiences in a fun, safe context. It is okay if a client only chooses "positive" feelings. The point is to simply help normalize the habit of describing feelings and experiences.

Tip: Drawing feeling faces can be surprisingly difficult at first. We recommend looking through your emojis on your phone before playing to get an idea of all the different feeling faces you can draw. If you play the game multiple times over the course of therapy, you may want to use more and more difficult feeling faces as you go.

Smell the Difference

Training young people to pay attention to their experience can be incredibly difficult when they have problems closing their eyes, practicing traditional mindfulness, or more generally lack the precision to identify private experiences. This exercise, inspired by Dixon's (2015) research on equivalence training, helps clients practice their noticing skills in a different way—through smell!

Materials

- Paper flowers (purchased or homemade)—alternatively, cotton balls work

- Essential oils or scented sprays

Clinician Note

Some children and adolescents may have asthma or allergies that can be exacerbated by oils or scents. Always check with their caregiver before proceeding with this exercise. If a child is sensitive to scents, you may want to use more natural scents like a freshly-cut orange or lemon rather than an oil or spray that can diffuse throughout the air.

Instructions

- Apply essential oil or scented spray to paper flowers or cotton balls (have at least *two different* smells).

- Place paper flowers some distance apart or store cotton balls in separate plastic baggies.

- Instruct your client to pick a flower or plastic baggie, and to smell it.

- Ask them to describe what they smell, noticing if any images pop up in their mind. Ask what the smell reminds them of or if they've ever smelled anything like it before.

- Invite them to set the flower or baggie aside as you debrief what they noticed.

- Have them pick up the next flower (or baggie with cotton ball), and instruct them to smell it.

- Again, prompt them to describe what they notice, specifically orienting them to describe the smell in any way available to them—such as images, thoughts, or memories that occur to them.

- You may end the exercise by instructing them to notice different smells they experience over the following week, and report back what they notice.

Web of Life

This experiential activity is about training a verbal repertoire, a way for the young people we work with to reference their implicit painful experiences and to talk about them, describing how they interact with them—making explicit the painful private experiences that have effects on one's behavior.

Materials

- Yarn—we like to use varying balls of yarn that are different colors and thicknesses

- Scissors to cut the yarn

- Paper and wide-tip markers

- Tape or clothespins (optional)

Instructions

- **Orient your young client by explaining:** "Having painful thoughts like: 'I'm not good enough,' 'I'll fail,' 'No one likes me,' or worrying about the future; painful feelings like sadness, anger, or worry; painful sensations, like a sick feeling in your stomach or physical pain or heart pounding; and painful memories, like remembering a time something awful happened to you, are all normal experiences. I have them too."

- **Describe how the exercise works:** "In this exercise we're going to use different pieces of yarn to represent our journey from one experience to another. Some are painful, some are important, and some are both!"

- **Complete this introduction by transitioning into what you will do in the exercise:** "We're going to untangle some of your experiences by creating a web of yarn. As we unroll the different pieces of yarn, they will overlap with other pieces going in different directions—creating a connected 'web' all over the office. I'll write down different experiences that you describe to me on these sheets of paper—painful, important, or both—and I'll hand them to you so that you can fasten them along the yarn at different spots."

- You may wish to give a specific instruction about how to use the yarn based on your context. You may have your young client tie yarn to various pieces of furniture so that the web hangs off the ground, or you may suggest the young client unroll the yarn on the floor if you do not have anything to tie the yarn to or are worried about knocking over furniture or decorative objects.

  ◦ In creating a web, some young people have opted not to tie or attach it at varying heights through our office, but instead lay out the web on the ground. Whatever works for your context and for the ability of your client is fine.

- Take time to work through this exercise. You may want to use different colors for different years or timelines in your client's life—be creative and encourage them to express their timeline and journey in any way that works for them.

- Once you have completed the web, with a number of different experiences marked on paper and fastened to the yarn, have the client stand back and notice their experience.

- Invite them to guide you through the web, following one length of yarn at a time, recounting their history and experience with this length of yarn.

- Be curious, asking questions about the web and how each string interacts with one another and how your client experiences that.

Counting Your Breath

This introductory mindfulness script is an exercise appropriate for all ages. This exercise is simply about orienting the young person's attention to the present moment. Encourage your client to notice any experience: positive ones, such as relaxation, or negative ones, such as distraction or boredom. The goal is not to experience a certain emotion or state, such as relaxation, but rather to *notice* whatever experience they have.

Script

"I'm going to teach you something simple that will help you learn to concentrate better. First, you'll need to sit up tall so that your back is straight. Rest your hands on your knees. Now, take an extra-long inhale—breathe all the way in. Pause for a moment and feel your breath. Exhale all the way out. Notice the sensations that change in your body as you breathe out. Say aloud or silently to yourself 'one.'

Let's repeat: Breathe in all the way, pause for a moment, then exhale and count 'two.'

Inhale all the way. Pause, noticing where you feel your breath in your body. Exhale. Breathe all the way out. Count 'three.'"

Debrief

Debrief this brief introduction to mindfulness by asking, "What did you notice?"

Avoid asking leading questions such as, "Did you feel relaxed?" or "Did your mind get quiet?" Instead, focus on training attention to any experiences that show up. Discuss any distractions that your client may have noticed. Remember, the purpose of training their attention is to *notice* what happens to their attention.

Adapting This Exercise

When working with younger children, we have found some benefit in holding up one finger when we count "one," two fingers when we count "two," and so on, and having our young client follow along.

Once you've successfully introduced this exercise, use it again in future sessions, but increase the count length up to 10. This can be a simple exercise they can also practice on their own or with guidance from their caregivers. If using it with caregivers, it is important to stress that the goal of this practice is *noticing* and to provide cues for how they should talk to the young person about the exercise, such as prompting, "What did you notice?" Without this explanation, caregivers may accidentally reinforce the idea that this exercise is meant for relaxation, which can lead to frustration for the client or caregiver when the client does not "relax" after practicing.

MAKING ACCEPTANCE AND MINDFULNESS EXPERIENTIAL

Fight Off the Balloons: Part 1

This next exercise focuses on acceptance of difficult experiences while incorporating aspects of mindfulness, values, and values-based behaviors, and helps to establish what our work is about. This exercise also tackles the idea of "fusion" that we discussed previously through helping young clients understand the idea that there is space between them and their thoughts and feelings; that they are not their thoughts and feelings, they simply experience them.

We have found this exercise helpful with young people who suffer with severe behavioral problems, such as acting out in anger. In one instance, working with a 10-year-old girl who was acting out at school—yelling at classmates, striking the teaching staff, and threatening suicide—this exercise promoted a different relationship with anger, encouraging her to notice anger and pay attention to how it impacted her behavior instead of simply reacting to the anger. This paying attention allowed her to develop new patterns of choosing how she would like to respond when anger showed up.

Fight Off the Balloons: Part 1

Materials

- Balloons: You will not require many balloons, but more balloons are more fun in our experience. You may already have the balloons inflated or may wish to inflate them in session with your client; however, the balloons need to be tied so that they remain inflated.

  - *Tip: You may need to inquire about whether your clients are sensitive to latex. We have found non-latex balloons online easily for a low price.*

- Markers (we recommend washable markers to minimize the chance of staining skin or fabrics)

Preparing the Balloons

- Have your client describe a difficult private experience (a thought, feeling, sensation, or memory) that they have been struggling with. For example: anger. Ask questions such as: "What does your mind tell you when you're angry?" or "Where do you feel anger in your body? What does it feel like?"

- Then, instruct your client to write the private experience on a balloon. You may wish to ask them to pick a balloon color for that private experience and a marker color. We've also had success instructing young clients to depict that private experience, drawing "anxiety" or "frustration" as a monster on a balloon.

- Pause and be purposeful in this activity, even articulating these painful experiences may be an improvement in behavior for your client.

- Try not to let your client get too caught up in the story about each of the private experiences. Smile and encourage participation, continuing with the writing and depiction of these painful private experiences rather than talking in that moment about where they come from or why they're happening.

Instructions

Use markers to write down words on the balloons that represent painful private experiences that your young client is experiencing—for example: *fear, worry, sadness, anger, panic, soreness, loss.* Alternatively, if the private experiences include memories or painful topics that are difficult to verbalize—including preverbal trauma—you can draw images and invite the young client to also draw images that represent the difficult private experiences. With drawing, the images need not be sophisticated. We have had a young client use multiple marker colors, creating a blob-like creature and smudging the image on the balloon to further depict its grotesqueness.

It is important to be flexible in session and notice what will reinforce pointing to difficult private experiences. Simply the act of identifying painful experiences and articulating them on the balloons could very well create an improvement in your young client's behavior and increase their psychological flexibility in that they are already learning a new way to relate to their painful experiences, especially as you, the therapist, model being okay with these difficult experiences.

With several inflated balloons now covered in words or decorated with images depicting the difficult private experiences for your young client, invite your client to stand apart from you. Holding up the balloons, remind your client that the balloons represent their difficult feelings, thoughts, sensations, and even memories that they don't want to have. Then say: "Now I'm going to throw these balloons at you. They can't hurt you, they're just balloons, but remember what they represent: the scary and yucky thoughts, feelings, memories, and sensations we put on them. I want you to try your best to not let these balloons touch you. You can fight off the balloons, you can do whatever you want—push them away, duck, roll, jump out of the way—but as I throw these at you, I am going to try and talk to you about something important. Will you try this with me?"

Then, begin vigorously throwing the balloons at your client, picking up spent balloons after they've been thrown. All the while, tell them about something important—like a pet you love very much or a really great movie you think your client will like.

After a minute or so of throwing the balloons, stop and ask: "What happened?" Listen as your young client talks about fighting off the balloons and running away; then ask, "How hard was that?" Regardless of your client's answer, orient them to how difficult it is to do other things while fighting off the scary and yucky stuff we don't want to have. Focusing more specifically, describe observable behaviors: "How well can you eat a piece of pizza while you're fighting off these yucky and scary thoughts? And if I wanted to teach you how to drive a car, can you do that while you're fighting these off?"

Be sure to take time to debrief this first part of the exercise fully, exploring what your young client's experience of the exercise is. Specifically, the aim is to have them understand that what they can do is limited when they attempt to fight off the balloons representing their painful experiences.

Fight Off the Balloons: Part 2

Part 2 repeats the activity of you throwing balloons at your young client with special instructions: "This time, we're going to do something slightly different. I want you to let the balloons hit you, and I am going to talk to you about something important. Ready?"

Repeat throwing the balloons at your young client, all the while repeating the same information from the previous round—speaking about something personally important, whether it be a pet or a movie you think your client will like. You may need to remind them that fighting or escaping the balloons is not necessary this time around.

Once you finish telling your young client about what was important, or simply after a minute of this exercise, ask: "How was that different from the first time?" Your client may answer in a variety of ways. Again, inquire of them how difficult it would be to do other things while not fighting off the yucky and scary stuff we don't want to have. Focusing more specifically, ask about observable behaviors, such as: "How well can you eat a piece of pizza when you're not fighting off the yucky and scary thoughts? And if I wanted to teach you how to drive a car, could you focus on that while you're just letting the balloons hit you and land wherever they may?"

This exercise is completed by drawing a distinction between fighting with our private experiences and allowing them to simply be there or touch us, highlighting acceptance through the client's own experiences with both rounds of the balloons.

Fight Off the Balloons for Groups

This group adaptation of the Fight Off the Balloons exercise is a fun and physical way of demonstrating the role of acceptance, values, and mindfulness in a young person's life. Facilitate a brief discussion about what is difficult for participants and encourage group participants to write down or depict the thoughts, feelings, sensations, and memories that come up with those difficulties on the balloons provided. For this adaptation, once you have collected a smattering of answers depicted across several balloons (the more the better), you will divide the group of young people you're working with into three teams:

Balloon Throwing Team. This should be the largest team. For example, in a group of 12 participants, we would assign half the group (six participants) to the Balloon Throwing Team. This team's job is to throw the balloons, pick them up, and keep throwing them at the Avoiding Balloons Team.

Avoiding Balloons Team. In a group of 12 young people, this team would be made up of four participants. Their job is to not let the balloons hit them, to essentially fight them off at all costs (running, jumping, pushing the balloons away, using objects as shields).

Values Cheerleaders. The third team, stands around the periphery of the room or space that the group is working in. Values Cheerleaders encourage the Avoiding Balloons Team to "come have fun" by asking them to do things that they might enjoy, such as: "Let's go play a game together!" or "Hey, want to go on a hike with me?" The Values Cheerleaders might ask the Avoiding Balloons Team, "Hey, are you okay?" or attempt to tell them something important: "I got a puppy today! His name is Goldie and he's a golden retriever. Want to meet him?"

Instructions

- Tell the Avoiding Balloons Team that for the first round, you want them to fight off the balloons. They can attempt to dodge them, hit the balloons away, and even try to hide or use an object as a shield.

- Tell the Balloon Throwing Team to relentlessly throw balloons at the Avoiding Balloons Team, picking up balloons and repeating this activity.

- Tell the Values Cheerleaders to try and connect from the sidelines with the Avoiding Balloons Team. They can call out, wave, etc., but they can't get in the way of the Balloon Throwing Team.

After the exercise is done, set the balloons aside and facilitate a brief discussion about what the group participants noticed. You may ask:

- "What did you notice?" or
- "What happened?"

Prompt the group to share what they noticed, specifically asking:

- "What happens when the Avoiding Balloons Team tries to fight off all their painful stuff?"
- "Do the balloons stop coming?"
- "How well can the Avoiding Balloons Team connect with the Values Cheerleaders?"

You might also be more directive, asking the Avoiding Balloons Team:

- "How well were you able to notice the things the Values Cheerleaders were saying to you?"

Instruct the group that you will do a second round, but this time the Avoiding Balloons Team will not fight off the balloons and instead notice what happens. They will notice what else they're free to do if they're not focused on avoiding balloons. Giving the same amount of time (at least a minute or two for the exercise to play out), have the Balloon Throwing Team throw balloons and the Values Cheerleaders attempt to connect with the Avoiding Balloons Team, but this time the Avoiding Balloons Team engages in different behaviors.

Upon completion of this activity, set the balloons aside, and be careful to debrief the specifics of what is different when the Avoiding Balloons Team chose not to fight their pain.

After having run this group with varying presenting concerns, as well as age demographics, if some young people protest the practice of acceptance in the pursuit of being flexible with what one does—for instance saying, "I can't just ignore my pain"—validate that response! We've had a lot of success by responding, "Exactly! If you try to ignore these painful balloons, you might try hard to focus on something pleasant, but that might not work for long. Instead we want to be sensitive to how these balloons influence how we behave in the moment!"

An Unwanted Guest

This script is an adaptation of a Hayes, Strosahl, and Wilson's (2011) metaphor on working with increasing willingness to feel painful content so that the practice of acceptance is more easily available. In this script, we encourage clients to recognize how their behavior works when they attempt to keep thoughts, feelings, sensations, or memories away. This script can easily be adapted as a discussion for situations where an activity may not be appropriate or workable. For example, in working with adolescents who are hesitant to engage in therapy or dismissive of the experience, more generally you might ask them a series of questions about how they might try to keep their unwanted guest out.

Script

"Imagine that you're having a party at home with friends or family members, people who are important to you, who you want to spend time with and whose company you enjoy. Imagine some of the activities you might do together—play a game, eat some good food, talk to one another and catch up on each other's lives.

There's a catch to this scenario. On the way to your party is an uninvited guest, someone who you don't want there. You know that if they show up, they'll really spoil your fun and generally ruin the good time you're having.

The moment that you learn about their impending arrival, you do your best to close the windows, shut the drapes or blinds, turn some of the lights down, lock the doors, and turn the music down. You turn your attention away from the people who are important to you and the things you could be doing with them in order to keep this unwanted, uninvited guest out.

Sadly, your efforts are thwarted by the simple fact that they knock loudly on the door, turn the handle, try to knock on the windows, and look in, shouting loudly.

Your guests are becoming curious about what is going on. You turn up some music and tell them not to worry about it and to have a good time. You've now spent several minutes attempting to distract everyone from what is really going on.

One of your guests forgot something in their car, or lives close by and needs to return home to get what they meant to bring. You know if they open the door, there's a chance this unwanted guest could get in, so you discourage them from leaving. When they do leave, you close the door quickly behind them but have to answer to this unwanted guest who insists, 'Hello! I've been knocking. Let me in.' Your guests notice and invite them in, much to your dismay.

As they start interacting with your guests, you try to get in their way or distract them; you try to change conversations quickly when the unwanted guest brings up a sore topic. Maybe you invite the unwanted guest into the kitchen to grab a snack and keep them occupied in there so they don't bother your friends or embarrass you, but it also means that you don't get to spend time with your friends."

Debrief

After going through the script, help your clients identify what is problematic about this strategy: They don't get to enjoy time with friends and family they care about because all of their attention is spent trying to keep the uninvited guest out.

Explain that our painful private experiences (thoughts, feelings, memories, and physical sensations) are like the uninvited guest—we don't want them there, but sometimes they show up anyway—and all the different ways we try to hide from them, make them go away, or keep them occupied by talking to them in our head, keep us from spending time with the people who matter most to us. What would it be like to let the uninvited guest in and still connect with your friends and family?

Escape Room

This game focuses on demonstrating for young clients how their mind works in both helpful and unhelpful ways. The game begins by showing them how they can *think* of ways to escape a room without interacting with anything in the room, they can simply sit and come up with viable answers.

Instructions

- Start this exercise by saying, "Imagine that our session is over today. You're happy with the work we've done here together and as we say our goodbyes, we get up, walk to the door, and try to leave but can't. The door handle just spins as we turn it; the lock is broken. How would we get out of this room? Notice any answers that your mind comes up with, even if they seem silly or over the top."

- Facilitate a discussion with your client based on all the different ways that they could attempt to escape the room: climbing out a window, banging loudly on the door and shouting for people on the other side to help, taking the hinges off the door, breaking the door down—what would they use? If they say to use a cell phone to call for help, ask, "Without even taking your cell phone out, is it charged? Who would we call? Would they answer? Do you have data on your phone to look up a local locksmith or another local business that could come over and try the door from the other side?"

- Then, you may explain the exercise to the client: "It might seem silly, thinking of all the ways we could get out of a locked room, even though our door is unlocked right now and we can leave at any time. The thing is that our minds are really good at coming up with answers, being creative, and imagining things. We didn't have to even experience being locked in a room for you to come up with a lot of great ways to help us escape. Sometimes, like if we were locked in a room, the ability of our minds to come up with answers is really helpful. But sometimes all it does is bring worries, ideas, or thoughts into this moment that aren't really helpful at all. It's our job to figure out when our mind is being helpful and when it's being unhelpful."

This can then lead into a discussion where the young client identifies things their mind does that are unhelpful and how they can tell the difference, or it can simply be a good way to reinforce concepts you have already discussed with your client previously.

PLANNING FIRST STEPS

Life Map

The Life Map is a tool we use in groups and with individual clients of all ages. This Life Map worksheet is specially designed for working with young people and helping them to not just identify their values and the behaviors they do that are in line with their values, but also in assisting them in identifying their painful experiences and what they do to escape pain. It normalizes avoidance attempts and trains them to notice what motivates their behavior by having them pay attention to what each direction, chasing their values and escaping pain, feels like. Remember, this ability to discriminate behavior under the control of values (in contrast to escaping pain) is essential to this approach.

We use the metaphor of a bunny who loves carrots and is afraid of dogs to help young people identify what their values and hooks are, and to point out that neither chasing values nor escaping pain is inherently good or bad, but that we want to be aware of what is driving our behavior and how it works so we have more control over what we choose to do.

For example, a bunny who *always* hides from barking dogs never gets to eat any delicious carrots and a bunny who *only* eats delicious carrots could be in big trouble if they aren't looking out for the barking dog.

As a final note, be cautious when using the Life Map to consider that both directions (chasing values and escaping pain) are understood as being helpful at times.

Life Map

What does it look like when you're chasing carrots? What do you want to be doing?

Who and what are the carrots in your life?

What's the difference between chasing carrots and running away from dogs? What is it like to move in each direction?

What do you do to try and escape that?

What makes chasing your carrots hard?

Delay Circuit

Clients who report self-harming thoughts may benefit from a reminder of different activities or strategies they can use when these thoughts pop up. The Delay Circuit Worksheet outlines different strategies (with space for them to write their own) that they can use to cope when these overwhelming thoughts arise.

Delay Circuit

When self-harming thoughts show up or you feel overwhelmed, try these strategies to get connected and slow down.

Jump Start Your System

Do jumping jacks

Splash cold water on your face

Go for a run or bike ride

Get physical with an exercise class or video

Get Your Mind Involved

Play a game with others or by yourself

Draw a picture or create art

Read a good book

Have a conversation with a loved one

Slow Down and Pause

Listen to calming music

Take a warm bath or hot shower

Do some simple stretches or yoga

Try some mindful breathing

Put on comfortable clothes and relax

Brave

Our goal in therapy is to help clients engage less with their inner bullies and more with the life they want to live. This worksheet helps clients assess what their treatment goals are: what living a life of meaning looks like for them. The Brave worksheet has clients identify behaviors they already do, or want to be doing, that require bravery.

Rather than focusing on feeling brave, the worksheet focuses on behaviors—what they would actually do. This is an important feature: tracking specific behaviors rather than focusing on simply feeling a certain way to accomplish a feat.

Brave
Finding Your Inner Strength

To be brave means to do something even if you feel scared or if it is really hard. What do you do when you're brave? Maybe you go to school, or raise your hand when the teacher asks a question, or talk to someone new. In each of the boxes, write down one way you are brave; then draw a picture in the space below of what this looks like to you.

Growing My Garden

Thinking about behavior change can be overwhelming at first. It's easy to focus on negatives: "It'll never happen because…" or "I'm not smart enough." This is part of why so many people struggle with developing new patterns of responding, especially in the presence of painful thoughts and feelings.

This worksheet makes the early steps of behavior change easier through metaphor: Your life is a garden. To see certain parts of your garden grow, you need to water them, and your attention is the watering can! The message becomes clear: **Pay attention to what you want to see grow**.

Clients may want to hang this worksheet on the fridge at home or tape it to the wall in their bedroom as a reminder of what they are working toward.

Growing
My Garden

Write down a behavior you want to work towards in the center of the flower and use each leaf to plan small steps to work to achieve it.

Holding What Hurts

Using tangible examples to demonstrate for young people how to be accepting and explain what the implications of living this way is a useful way of getting buy-in early on in your therapeutic work. In our experience, teens and children are some of the most skeptical consumers of therapy. We theorize this is generally because they can control most things in their lives, or their caregivers can.

We used this exercise with great success with an adolescent male who was convinced that he could figure out how to not be socially anxious anymore—his solution was solving his body image dissatisfaction. His statement to us was, "If I just looked good, I'd be fine. All my problems would be gone." He fantasized about surgeries that would cure his physical appearance; he sobbed and advocated that his parents should figure out how to convince health professionals that he needed elective surgeries to make him look better.

The strength of his advocacy extended to demonstrating in very sound arguments how times had indeed changed: Social media impacted the lives of young people in such a profound way and looking the way he did was a considerable hindrance.

This Holding What Hurts exercise was an important early breakthrough for this young client to begin slowing down into the pain he was long struggling against.

Holding What Hurts

Materials

We recommend using a burr that you might find from a plant, a small piece of cactus, or even using a small crosscut saw. Truly, anything that has sharp edges but isn't dangerous to hold onto will do.

Instructions

- Show the burr or sharp item you will be using as an example to your client.

- Demonstrate, using your own hand, how this object is not *very* dangerous—you can hold it in your hand (without pressing down).

- Explain that the item you're holding in your hand is just like the pain that your client is dealing with: "This burr is just like what hurts you about your body image. It represents all these painful thoughts and feelings you have about your own body."

- While holding the burr or sharp item, demonstrate how holding this pain isn't inherently problematic and doesn't cause any long-term damage. You can roll it in your palm, or hold your hand out flat and let this sharp object sit there.

- Demonstrate how fighting against this burr or sharp object can lead to more pain, just as battling with their private pain can add to their suffering. Perhaps you begin to close your fingers around the sharp object. (This is why we elect to use a burr or small piece of cactus—we can generally get away with clenching it for a few seconds without it puncturing our skin to show that this is indeed painful but not seriously injurious.)

- Show your client how pushing against this sharp item can similarly lead to more pain.

- Invite them to hold their hand out flat and place this burr or sharp object in their hand.

- Ask them to notice what it's like to hold this pain in their hand without fighting against it.

- Prompt your client to pay special attention to the weight of the object in their hand and to notice that they can indeed feel it there in their hand—it's very much present in their world but that it doesn't govern *how* they live their life; it doesn't rule them.

- Ask the young person you're working with what doing this, holding their pain, might mean in their life. Specifically, ask them what they could do if they allowed this pain to be in their life. Who would it matter to? What would be made possible by not overtly battling with this pain?

Just as in previous exercises, the debrief of this exercise can be just as valuable as the exercise. Rather than some intellectual understanding of simply what it means to be accepting or to practice acceptance, we wish to highlight the real-world implications of being accepting.

Explicitly take time to ask your young client: "If I was hanging out with you or just following you around in your daily life, outside of this office, and you were holding what hurts, not fighting it, what would I see you doing? How would I know you're living what we just did here?"

Follow up their response with a question that connects this concept to some potentially valuable life domains:

- Why would that matter to you?
- What would it impact in your world?
- Who would this make a difference to?

The goal is to first help clients understand what acceptance is, but then also see what acceptance may look like in their life in terms of real-world behaviors.

Conceptualization with Young People

In working from an acceptance and mindfulness framework, we worry that important clinical operations, such as writing assessment reports and case conceptualization, fall by the wayside. While the vast majority of the worksheets and exercises in this book are to be used by the client or caregiver, this worksheet is designed to be completed by you, the mental health professional. It is an opportunity to conceptualize your client's values, hooks, patterns of avoidance, and treatment goals.

It can be helpful to take time and look at your client's full experience, and make sure you both are on track with your treatment plan. This is an adaptation of a worksheet found in *The ACT Approach* (Gordon & Borushok, 2017).

Connect
with Function

Part 1: Give at least one answer in each section

3. When those private experiences show up, what do they do to try and avoid or escape them?

4. What behaviors does your client want to begin or do more of that takes them towards their values?

_____ _____

2. What thoughts, feeling, memories, or physical sensations show up that get in the way of what is important to them?

1. Who and what is important to your client? What qualities or characteristics does your client want to be about?

Part 2: Notice your experience

What does it feel like for YOU, the therapist, to take a step back and observe the patterns of avoidance for your client? Have you and your client already answered all of these questions together in session? Do the goals of treatment match what the diagram above says?

Treatment and Skill Building

ACCEPTANCE AND MINDFULNESS

Activities in this chapter help to build specific skills. These are the new ways of working with the difficult content that shows up in a young person's world. The goal of this chapter is to bring to life the practice of acceptance and mindfulness, regardless of the situation. We will present you with skills, scripts, and exercises/activities (including group practices, therapeutic art, and worksheets) for you to implement.

You do not need to rigidly adhere to the structure we have; you can adapt it to be workable for your clients and the situations you find yourself practicing in. For example, many of our worksheets can be adapted to a whiteboard or a discussion depending on what works best for the client and situation.

Breathing on Purpose

This mindfulness exercise is designed to help you implement mindfulness in a playful way with the young people you work with. In our experience, this exercise is appropriate for all age levels and you can easily use it with groups as well.

Script

"You may wish to close your eyes if you're comfortable with that. If not, go ahead and allow your vision to drop and gaze to soften so that you're not intently focusing on one thing but just letting the muscles around your eyes relax.

Let's begin by taking a breath on purpose. Really pay attention to the sensations when you breathe in. Notice what it's like to be here, now. Are you feeling relaxed, antsy, bored? Whatever shows up, notice that you're feeling something.

Let's breathe in all the way and then out all the way. [*Model breathing in and then out.*]

Let's see if we can repeat that, but making our breath more audible this time. [*Model breathing in and out audibly.*]

Inhaling and then exhaling all the way out is one full breath.

Take three breaths in your own time and be aware of anything that happens while you breathe. Notice if your mind has anything to say about what you're doing right now, any judgments or reactions. Really pause and listen to what your mind has to say about this experience of breathing on purpose—whether it's good, bad, or indifferent. Your job is to simply notice what your mind does as we breathe.

Before we end this exercise, let's take one last breath on purpose together, pausing here to notice what it's like to be in this moment right now."

Mindful Breathing for Children

This adaptation of our Breathing on Purpose exercise is one that we have found especially helpful with children when we're working to train them on paying attention to their experience with mindfulness.

Script

"From a comfortable, seated posture, or laying down on your back, let your body be still. If you're comfortable, you may wish to close your eyes. If not, try not to focus on anything in the room. Let your vision be soft, not focusing on any one thing.

Take a breath on purpose, breathing all the way in. Notice what it feels like to breathe in and out right now.

Place a hand on your belly and feel how the belly lifts as you breathe in and drops as you breathe out.

Move a hand up to your chest. Ask yourself if you can feel your chest moving or heart beating as you breathe.

Place a finger close to your nostrils, take an extra deep breath in on purpose and feel the air rush past your finger. Breathe out all the way and feel the air once again rush past your finger. Notice how the inhale, breathing in, and exhale, breathing out, each have different sensations on your finger.

Letting your hand rest, see if you can notice the difference in temperature of the air that you breathe. Cool air on the inhale and warm air on the exhale.

Before we end this exercise, take a moment to wiggle your fingers, rotate your wrists, roll your shoulders up—forward and down. Move your head from side to side. And in your own time, open your eyes and refocus your attention on us working together.

What did you notice? Could you feel different sensations: your belly, chest, heart, breath on your finger? Could you notice the different temperature of the air? Did you get distracted at all?"

Hands-on Breathing

This mindful breathing activity bridges highly engaging physical exercises with slower, inward-focused meditation. We find that this engaging form of mindful breathing is most helpful with young people who have difficulties maintaining their attention and find themselves easily distracted with traditional mindfulness exercises.

Script

"Get seated comfortably so that you won't have to move or adjust for a few minutes.

While we're sitting here, take a breath on purpose, breathing all the way in. Notice what that feels like in your body.

Place your hands over your chest and take another breath, feeling your hands move as you breathe. Check to see if that feels any different than breathing without your hands on your chest.

Move your hands down to your belly and take another breath. Breathe into your belly, pressing your hands against your stomach and noticing the movement under your hands. As you inhale, the belly becomes larger, moving your hands out; and then as you exhale the belly deflates, lowering your hands—like holding a balloon that is inflated and deflated over and over again.

Moving your hands down your legs, wrap your palms around your knees and, without changing anything, just breathe normally and see how that feels.

Reach your hands around behind you, placing them on your back, and take a breath on purpose. See if you can feel any sensations of breathing in your hands. Can you feel the breath moving in your back at all?

Before we end, lower your hands and hold one finger under your nose like a mustache—floating it above your upper lip. Breathing through your nose only, take a breath on purpose and notice the sensations of air rushing past your finger. Pause to see what you notice as you breathe. Notice the difference in temperature as you inhale and exhale—warm air as you breathe out and cool air as you breathe in."

End this exercise with a debrief of what they noticed. Remember to be extra reinforcing if they noticed their attention drift—that means they were successful at paying attention to their experience. As your clients master this brief mindfulness activity, extend its duration to two or three breaths, working your way up to five or 10 breaths for each position.

Slo-Mo Yoga

This yoga exercise encourages your young clients to focus their attention by moving slowly, in sync with their breathing.

Script

"From a comfortable seated or standing posture, inhale while *slowly* lifting your arms up, taking the full length of your inhale to do so.

With your arms in the air, exhale, letting a long breath out while pressing through the tips of your fingers, reaching higher with your arms, and lengthening through your spine to sit tall but not rigid.

Inhale and raise your vision, looking up past your fingers.

As you exhale, bend forward at your hips until your chest is parallel with your legs, lowering your arms as you breathe out, allowing your arms to dangle and your head to rest in a comfortable, loose position.

Press your hands into your shins if standing, or knees if seated.

Take the full length of your inhale to return to an upright position, until your arms are extended and you are looking forward.

Exhale slowly and bend forward again, your arms relaxed.

Inhale, and slowly return to an upright seated or standing position.

Take the full length of your exhale to lower your arms and come to rest.

Repeat several times."

Once your clients master this exercise, invite them to guide you both through the exercise.

Yoga for Anxiety, Stress, and Anger

Mindfulness meditation can be difficult for young people. Those who are more cynical might think that meditation is simply about closing one's eyes and pretending to look serious. We don't blame them! The effects of mindfulness are profound, but learning this skill can be difficult for many. Therefore, we've long suggested using embodied mindfulness, using movement as a way of training present-moment awareness (Gordon, 2013).

Script

"Lying with your body flat on the earth, feel the breath that's moving your body at this moment. Notice where you feel that movement of breath: in the belly, the chest. Maybe you even feel the sensations of air rushing past your nostrils.

Just feel how your body moves with your breath, without trying to make it any different than it is. Breathe, be in this moment, in your body, on this earth.

Notice if you feel your body sinking down, becoming heavier with your next exhalation, and possibly feeling some lightness or buoyancy or softness on the inhalation.

With as much ease and as slowly as you can, begin to roll your head side to side against the earth with your breath. Take the full length of your exhale to move it to one side and the full length of your inhale to come back to center with your head, then moving it to the other side with the next exhale.

Pay attention to anything you're noticing: thoughts, feelings, sensations, memories. And notice the contact of your head with the earth. Notice where your head touches the ground and what those sensations are like.

Notice the movement of your neck, possibly even a sense of the neck muscles as you move from side to side. Softening your jaw, allow the muscles around your mouth to relax. Perhaps the teeth unclench, and the lips may even separate.

Soften the muscles around your eyes. Come back to center with your head on your next inhale. Notice the weight of your body pressing down; feel what your breath is like in this moment.

As though you could travel from your head down your neck to your upper back, pay attention to how your body feels on the ground. With your breath, begin to lift your arms up, straight above you with your fingers pointing to the sky.

Take a breath here on purpose. On your next breath, lengthen through the fingers, as if you were reaching for the ceiling, fingers extending upward.

On your next exhalation, with your arms and fingers still extended, soften the muscles around your shoulders, dropping your shoulders down to the floor. Move softly and gently. Notice the movement of the shoulder blades away from the spine as your fingers point up.

As you exhale, allow your arms to slowly drop back toward the floor. Find any position for your arms that works for you—bent or straight, anything that takes it easy on your neck and shoulders.

Be aware of your breath here. On your next exhalation, draw your knees in toward your chest, wrapping your arms above or under your knees. Then, rock from side to side, giving yourself a little yoga hug here.

Moving with the breath, let your shoulders drop back and your head become heavy. Just let your head lay flat against the earth.

Notice your breath here and how your breath changes as you move, as you change position, and connect with the wisdom of that change.

Keep your left knee drawn in toward your chest and bring your right foot flat to the floor with a nice bend to the knee. Or extend your right leg along the floor, pushing the heel away gently, flattening the foot out.

Take a breath here. Notice what it's like to be in this moment with your body. Bring your left foot onto your right leg, your right hand on your left knee, and slowly spiral-twist your body to the right. Move slowly enough that you can feel what's happening through your hips. Feel your breathing as you move. Wherever your knees are, wherever they land, is fine.

Now release, so you are once again flat on your back. Let both your legs extend on the floor for a moment. This is what it feels like to lay on the earth, to stretch your legs out long and to just own this moment. You don't need to do anything else in this moment but be with yourself, to feel your breath, being here on purpose.

Notice whatever shows up as you breathe—perhaps some asymmetry of feeling, like the left side feels a little bit different than the right in some way. Maybe your mind is coming up with a judgment: "My one leg feels longer than the other!"

Be with what you notice. Pay attention to it. Take a breath on purpose to breathe in everything you've become aware of.

And when you're ready, with an inhale draw your right knee up toward your chest. With your left leg still extended, check the comfort of your lower back. If you notice tension, bring the left foot to the floor, bringing a bend to your left knee. If your left leg is extended, press through your heel; if your knee is bent, press through the bottom of your foot. Notice the sensations as you do this. Notice how your body responds.

Take it easy as you lengthen up through your torso, feeling the weight of your shoulders and your head. Bring your right foot onto your left leg, your left hand coming to rest on your right knee for a slow and gentle twist.

Notice the sensation of moving. Let your body rest where it does. Then come back to center again, with your back flat on the floor, both legs extended out. Take a breath on purpose; breathe all the way in and out.

Take a moment to just feel your body, your breath. Bend your knees and bring your feet back to the floor, feet pressed flat. Rock your knees from side to side. Really notice the range of movement in this rocking. Go slowly, moving in such a way that you don't have to shift your weight from one side to the other. Your back isn't involved in this motion, it stays flat on the floor, so it's only your knees moving slowly from side to side. Don't worry about doing something specific, this is your time to practice. To just notice your experience.

Take your time to roll over onto one side and pause. Take one last breath here on purpose. Feel what it's like to be in this moment.

When you feel ready, use an arm to prop yourself up; go slowly, returning to this space we share together. Preparing ourselves to resume the activities of our day."

Yoga for Depression, Sadness, and Grief

In contrast to the previous mindful movement exercise—where we use yoga for anxiety and stress to slow down and practice present-moment awareness—this script encourages a more energizing practice and can be helpful for young clients who present as lethargic, apathetic, or unfocused.

Once you feel comfortable with each of the yoga scripts, you may wish to combine them, starting with this script and finishing with the Yoga for Anxiety, Stress, and Anger script as one long practice. We find it particularly useful to begin our sessions with this combination when our young clients seem to be distracted, as the active script helps them to focus and pay attention to their bodies, while the previous slowing down script helps set the tone for moving forward with the session.

Script

"Sitting in your chair, feel your body sit up tall, as if a string attached to the top of your head is pulling you up. Try to soften your body even as you sit up tall.

Notice your breath flow in and out.

The next time you breathe in, reach your arms up to the sky and follow the movement with your gaze, so your eyes are looking up toward your hands.

Notice your breath flow in and out.

As you breathe out, bend all the way forward until your stomach touches the tops of your legs and your hands reach toward the floor, maybe even touching the floor if you can.

Notice your breath flow in and out.

Place your hands on the floor or on your shins. Take a breath in, straightening your back as you return to an upright position. Look forward as you pause here.

Then, as you breathe out, let your body relax and fold forward again. Notice if there are any changes to your breath flowing in and out.

On the next breath in, sit up and bring your arms above your head so your fingertips are pointing to the sky. Looking up past your fingers, stretch out your fingers like they're branches growing up towards the sun. Bring your hands together, the palms of your hands pressed against each other (like you are giving yourself a high five), and then bring your hands down so your thumbs touch your chest, with your hands still together.

Notice your breath flow in and out."

Repeat this sequence without the breath in and out in between segments so it becomes one smooth, continuous movement.

Rising Tide
Mindfulness Training

This playful variation on a mindfulness of breath exercise is meant to train young people to pay attention to their breath. Let's be frank for a moment, training adults to be mindful of their breath can be near impossible, let alone young people who may not see the utility of mindfulness or therapy in general!

We offer this fun way of directing attention to the breath with the aim of training specific behaviors in a young person: present-moment attention and commitment to practicing this work.

For this activity, you can encourage a young client to picture a boat placed on top of their upper abdomen—the region below the nipples but above the belly button. When possible, we recommend using a toy boat, as we have had success even with hyperactive children when they have a physical object to focus on. Alternatively, you may wish to use any other type of safe, lightweight object and adapt this exercise.

Script

"Let's lay flat on our backs. Look forward and picture [*or physically place*] a toy boat on top of your belly.

The crew of this boat is in training, just like us. We're going to help them by giving them different kinds of waves to deal with so that they can learn how to pilot their boat.

Let's just lay still and breathe normally. Notice that the boat doesn't lift very much or drop very far. This is what calm water is like. The waves just move smoothly. The boat gently rocks forward as we inhale, just like a wave is coming toward it and raising it up. And gently the boat leans downward as we exhale. The wave has passed and for a short time the boat is flat, before the next wave comes.

Now, let's simulate a big wave: Breathe in all the way, filling your belly with air, and watch the boat rise up high. This is a BIG wave.

Pause here with your belly full of air. The wave is so big it's carrying the boat. See if you can breathe in a little deeper. The boat's crew is dealing with this wave and getting ready for what comes next.

Slowly breathe all the way out, letting the boat down gently. Remember the boat's crew is still learning how to deal with these big waves. We don't want to sink them. Yet! [*If the boat falls off, tell your client, "That's okay! Sometimes accidents happen. The crew all had life vests on and we'll give them another chance."*]

Let's repeat the slow breathing a few times. Breathe all the way in, feeling the belly expand. Pause for a moment. Take an extra breath in; then breathe all the way out, nice and slow.

Okay, the crew is ready, let's give them some rougher water. Breathe in quickly and exhale slowly. Notice what happens to the boat as you breathe, how its speed changes, lifting quickly and dropping down.

Notice what happens in your body. If you start to feel dizzy, you can stop and breathe normally. The boat's crew will give you a break.

After a few more breaths, let your breathing return to normal.

Good job! You taught the crew how to handle smooth water, big waves, and rough water.

What did you notice during that activity?"

Mindful Eating

Children and adolescents learn from their environment, and, unfortunately, our cultural environment is one of mindless eating and scarfing down food. A great way to practice mindfulness both in session and at home with caregivers is through mindful eating. This exercise can work really well with a small piece of candy, chocolate, or some food the child really loves because it can be naturally reinforcing to complete the exercise. We adapted this mindful eating exercise from *Master Guide to Stress* (Borushok, 2018).

Script

"Take the food and hold it (or the plate it is on) in your hand. Is it cool, neutral in temperature, or warm to the touch? Is it soft or firm?

Look at it closely. Is it uniform in color? Uneven? Flawed or unflawed? Is there a noticeable pattern or design on it?

Does it make any sound as you hold it or move it between your fingers?

Examine the food as if you've never encountered it before. Wonder about it—what is it? Where did it come from? How was it made or grown?

Smell the food. Does it have a scent, or is it odorless?

Notice any urges to eat it. Do you have any sense of impatience, thoughts, feelings, or desires? Does your mouth fill with saliva?

Be aware of your conscious decision to eat this food. Note any thoughts or feelings. Do you feel any sense of excitement?

Put the food in your mouth and let it rest on your tongue. What does it taste like before you bite down? What is the texture like? How does it feel on your tongue? Is it rough or smooth? Does it taste sweet or salty?

Bite into the food. Chew it slowly. How does the flavor change? Does it make a sound as you bite into it? Is the texture the same? What does your tongue do to move the food around in your mouth as you chew? Notice how it moves the food and keeps it in place for chewing.

Does this food evoke any feelings or memories? Practice being aware of the distinctions between the sensations in the moment and all the thoughts and feelings evoked by the act of eating. [*Maybe they remember the last time they had this food or where they were.*]

After swallowing, pause to notice any changes in the sensations of hunger or satisfaction of your appetite.

Once you've finished eating the food, pause and reflect on the experience. Notice any thoughts of 'wanting more' or any feelings of 'having enough.' What else can you be aware of before you transition to your next activity?"

No One Likes Burnt Popcorn Mindfulness Training

Throughout this chapter, we've been approaching mindfulness in a playful and somewhat unorthodox way: focusing on training present-moment attention rather than attempting miraculous feats of relaxation or nonjudgment. This mindfulness exercise is one we typically do in groups; however, we have had great success in individual practice settings due to its evocative and directly applicable nature. Every experience is an opportunity to cultivate the practice of mindfulness.

Materials

We really like to use burnt popcorn because almost no one likes burnt popcorn. Yes, we're sure a few of you will email us to say you, yourself, or your spouse likes the burnt kernels. That's fine, but you're outliers! In the past, we've used black licorice because a lot of people have a distaste for it, but it was too frequent that there would be that one child or adolescent in our groups who'd be throwing the black licorice back saying, "Oh I love these."

We recommend having a small cup with a small handful of popcorn for yourself and each young person you're working with if you're doing this exercise in a group.

Instructions

- Have the burnt popcorn already prepared in a small cup.

- Pass out a cup of burnt popcorn to each participant and yourself with the special instruction to leave the cup alone for now.

- Inform your young clients that, in this exercise, you're going to invite them to smell, touch, and eat the burnt popcorn.

- Pause to notice their reaction and, before responding, ask them to notice if they're having any thoughts about doing this exercise already.

- Instruct your clients to pay attention to whatever thoughts might be showing up for them, taking stock of how they're feeling or thinking, and to return to this moment by taking a breath on purpose.

- Invite them to begin by peering into the cup and noticing whatever shows up for them.

- Ask them to go slowly and carefully notice what occurs to them about the way the cup or popcorn looks, asking what stands out to them.

- Encourage them to hold the cup up to their face and smell the popcorn before they eat it.

- Invite intentional pausing and reflecting on whatever may arise, including thoughts such as, "This is weird." Be reinforcing; the point is that they're noticing.

- Invite your clients to now pick up a piece of burnt popcorn and to eat it, noticing its flavor on the tongue and any sensations as they bite into it and eat it.

Extra Sips of Air Mindfulness Training

This mindfulness of breath activity is one that we find highly engaging and useful with clients who feel stuck practicing mindfulness. This exercise challenges the young people you work with to manipulate their breathing, which requires a level of focus and effort that can be useful in helping clients to engage in the exercise and not be so caught up in their mind or distractions that can make mindfulness difficult for them.

Script

"Sit down in a comfortable position. If it's comfortable for you, you may wish to close your eyes. If that's not comfortable, go ahead and let your vision drop, allowing your eyes to go out of focus. Take a breath on purpose.

Notice the sensations of breathing, how the belly expands on an inhale and collapses on an exhale. Really pay attention to where you feel the breath moving in your body.

Notice how the chest lifts as you breathe in and drops as you breathe out. See if you can focus your attention to stay with the movement of your breath in your body.

Inevitably, distractions will arise, whether it's a sound, a sensation in your body (such as your nose itching), or tension in your body. That's okay. Whenever distractions arise, notice them. They're inevitable.

Come back to your breathing, noticing the sensations of your breath moving in your body.

On your next inhale, notice that there's a space between inhales and exhales. You breathe in and there's a brief pause, almost as if your body knows when it's full of air, followed by an exhale. See if you can catch that brief pause.

On your next inhale, breathe in, feel that pause, hold it for a moment and breathe in a little deeper, such as taking an extra sip of air, topping off the lungs with oxygen. Then, breathe all the way out. Notice what that feels like in your body.

Repeat that at your own pace a few times: breathing in, feeling the pause, taking an extra breath in, and exhaling all the way.

Still breathing here, allow your distractions to come: thoughts, sensations. And allow your distractions to go as you bring your attention back to the breath.

Before we end this exercise, take a brief moment to notice what it feels like to be in this moment.

Still with your eyes closed, bring your attention back to the room you're in. Notice the sounds in your environment and the sensations of the chair underneath your body.

Bring a little motion into the body: wiggling the fingers, rotating the wrists, maybe rolling the shoulders up, forward and down, moving the head from side to side, bringing some motion into the neck, allowing your body to wake up and meet this moment.

And when you feel ready, gently allow your eyes to open.

What did you notice?"

Flip Side of the Same Experience

This art activity is designed to help your young clients to recognize that the painful private experiences they struggle with are connected to their values—the people, things, and qualities most important to them.

Materials

You could simply use a piece of paper and a pencil, but we like to use art materials and a large piece of thick paper to make this activity more engaging and expressive artistically.

Instructions

- You may wish to begin with a brief settling-in exercise (a guided mindfulness exercise or yoga practice) to get present with whatever your client may be noticing.

- Instruct your client to start this exercise by simply looking at the page you're working with.

- Ask them to imagine that one side of the page represents the pain that shows up in their life: thoughts that they've struggled with, difficult feelings they've tried to avoid, memories they've wanted to forget, or sensations that have made their life hard.

- Encourage them to vividly imagine the ways in which this difficult stuff has impacted their lives. Ask: What has it cost them? What have they missed out on because of this pain?

- Have them decorate one side of the page with words and drawings that represent all of the pain they just told you about.

- Now, ask them to imagine that the other side of the page represents their values: the people and things that are most important in their lives.

- Have them decorate this second side of the page with words or drawings that represent the who and what that matter most to them, as well as qualities or characteristics they want to be about.

- Have them look at both sides and explain that values are the natural flip side of pain, explaining that it's reasonable that the things that hurt the most are connected to what matters the most. Help them identify this concept through examples of what they drew (maybe they drew themselves sad and alone on one side, and happy with their friends or family on the other).

- Alternatively, you may opt for a simpler iteration of this exercise by having your client simply use words to write about their pain on one side and the values that the pain is connected with on the opposite side.

Touch-Breathe-Sort-Repeat

Assisting young people in developing and reinforcing their intentional, focused attention is made fun and novel with this activity where we offer items of different textures, shapes, weight, sizes, and temperatures to sort.

Materials

- Two or more small buckets for sorting items.

- At least 10 small objects that can be hand held (two consistent variations at minimum). For example, you might use two different sized toy construction bricks: one rectangular shaped and the other cube shaped. Uncooked items also work (pasta, rice, kidney beans, lentils, etc.), or coins (perhaps two the same shape but one heavier).

- Sleep mask or other makeshift blindfold. Clients who feel uncomfortable or unsafe with a cover over their eyes may simply close their eyes, but watch out for cheating.

We recommend that you prepare this activity in advance by having the items used for sorting pre-mixed into a small bucket.

Instructions

- Explain to your client that this activity is meant to help them get really good at paying attention to different experiences and how they might be relating to them.

- Tell them that this activity involves several buckets: two of them are empty and one is full.

- Show them the contents of the full bucket, demonstrating that it's safe and not full of something gross or scary.

- Show how the remaining empty buckets are for sorting, and put one bucket on their left and the other on their right so they can sort easily.

- Offer your client a blindfold, or they can choose to close their eyes during the activity.

- Begin the exercise by inviting them to begin sorting by similar shape or size (i.e., rectangular pieces go in one box and square in the other).

- End the exercise when they have completed sorting or appear to become disinterested.

- Ask what they noticed as they were doing the exercise, eliciting any feedback they may have. Then ask specifically how focusing on their sensations of touch is different than sight alone.

- Finish by describing that there are many ways of knowing what we experience: through thinking, feeling, sensing, and remembering. Learning to slow into experiences can be a great benefit in understanding our reactions. You may want to transition this activity into some experience they have described in the past and have them try to describe the experience using all of their ways of knowing.

As your client advances in this activity, you may wish to increase the number of objects you have them sort, or have them sort objects not just by size or shape but by weight, texture, or similarity.

Life Map

In the previous chapter, we described the Life Map worksheet and explained how it can be useful for both conceptualization, as well as explicitly creating a therapeutic contract about growing behavior toward one's values, rather than focusing on escaping pain. We use the same format of the Life Map here, but rather than creating a map from scratch, we sort experiences in a discrimination training game.

Materials

- This game requires an oversized Life Map game board with four clearly labeled categories. This can be accomplished with four pages of printer paper and the following phrases written on the corresponding sheets:

  ◦ "It's Important!" (bottom right quadrant)

  ◦ "Watch Out!" (bottom left quadrant)

  ◦ "Run Away!" (top left quadrant)

  ◦ "Let's Do It!" (top right quadrant)

- In the middle we have a cartoon meditator depicted. You can also have your client draw themselves in the center or someone else meditating.

- A timer.

- Various cards for your client to sort. We have provided you with sample text for cards on the following page, but we suggest you tailor these cards to your client—removing those that
are irrelevant and adding cards manually that are relevant to the young person's life. These can be written on index cards, sticky notes, or cut-up pieces of paper.

  Remember to have instances of positively reinforcing people, things, and life events specific to the young client you're working with, as well as their unique aversive content (painful thoughts, feelings, sensations, and memories).

Instructions

You will hold the cards and control a timer. Once the timer starts, you will begin handing cards to your client, who will need to sort each card into one of the four categories. Each round of the game lasts until the cards have all been sorted. We have had a lot of success (and fun) having each of the four categories spread out so that our clients must move around a larger area to sort each of the cards.

Instruct your client that the point of this game is to get through as many cards as possible, sorting them correctly in their category before time is up. Remember, the definition of correct is different for each young person. The family card could just as easily go in the "It's Important!" category as it could be sorted into "Watch Out!" The experience of sorting is simply about taking the time to do the discrimination task and paying attention to the experience.

We end each round of the game by going through each of the cards that were sorted and having our client explain why they sorted each into the category they chose. For each card that they describe their sorting, we award them a point.

A quick note about debriefing the cards that were sorted: It's easy to get caught up in a verbal analysis of *why* a young person chose to put the cards in a certain category—this isn't incorrect, but don't be excessive. Remember, it's a game that we want to be reinforcing. Answers such as, "I don't know," might get a second prompt from us, "Well, what do you think about this card?" before we simply move on and ask about the next card in the pile.

Be flexible and creative in your scoring so that this game is reinforcing to your young client. You may want to track their score over multiple sessions, comparing their current score with their score during the last session. You can also award multiple tiers of prizes for higher scores.

Sample Text for Cards

Family	Staying Home from School	Time with Friends
Cuddling	Sad	Laughing
Playing Video Games	Crying	Singing
Not Sharing	Sharing	Being Proud
Dancing	Yelling	Eating Dessert
Feeling Scared	Arguing	Hugging
Hitting	High-Fiving	Secret Handshakes
Name Calling	Watching Movies	Making Fun of Someone
Eating	Hiding	
Drawing	Feeling Mad	

Inside or Outside?

Teaching young people to pay attention to their experiences can be explicit and relatively easy. We recommend you start simple and be reinforcing at first. Remember, we want to increase the chance that young people will continue to play along with our strange acceptance and mindfulness activities.

With this fun activity you will be training a discrimination task, contrasting what's happening inside your client—the private behavior that is only observable by your client:

- Their thoughts: the things they think, including judgments

- Feelings: the emotional content such as sadness, joy, worry, or fear

- Any sensations they notice from physical pain, the temperature of their feet, hunger pangs, itches, or soreness

- Memories, like images that occur to them, remembering a specific moment, and recalling a sensation

This worksheet can also be adapted to use as an in-session exercise where you ask your client to describe different, small objects you have in your office (outside) and also notice thoughts, memories, feelings, or sensations they have related to the objects (inside).

Inside
outside

This worksheet is all about identifying what is happening inside your mind and what you can notice with all five senses. Pick any item you can find at home and write down what you notice about the object and then what thoughts or judgments you have about the object. See the example of the yellow crayon below.

Object: Yellow Crayon

Write down everything you see, smell, feel, or hear about the object. Don't taste it!

Write down your thoughts, judgments, and/or evaluations about the object.

—— OUTSIDE ——

The crayon is yellow. The end is smudged because I used it to draw a picture yesterday. It smells like all the other crayons. The crayon fits in my hand. The paper around the crayon is rough, but the crayon is smooth.

—— INSIDE ——

I like the color yellow, but blue is my favorite color. I remember the last time I used this crayon I drew a picture of the sun. This crayon is the perfect size for my hand. I want to draw a picture of my dog today. My dog makes me happy and she's yellow.

Inside
outside

This worksheet is all about identifying what is happening inside your mind and what you can notice with all five senses. Pick any item you can find at home and write down what you notice about the object and then what thoughts or judgments you have about the object.

Object: _____

Write down everything you see, smell, feel, or hear about the object. Don't taste it!

Write down your thoughts, judgments, and/or evaluations about the object.

—— OUTSIDE ——

—— INSIDE ——

Sifting Experiences

Materials

- Four buckets or boxes, each labeled:

  ○ Sensations

  ○ Memories

  ○ Feelings

  ○ Thoughts

- A timer.

- Index cards or pieces of paper cut down into smaller rectangles.

- A plastic sifter or bucket.

Instructions

Each round of the game lasts for 60 seconds. We play one or two rounds of this game before sharing appreciations at the end of each session, tallying the score, and letting our young clients pick a reward from the treasure box.

Before beginning the game, we have clients create "Inside" cards. Using index cards or cut pieces of paper, have your client write down different thoughts, feelings, memories, and physical sensations they experience. These can include pleasant, unpleasant, and neutral experiences. If you have completed a Life Map with your client before, you may want to have them write down what was written in the bottom left quadrant on the cards.

If, for example, your client only lists feelings, but doesn't say any sensations, this can also be a good opportunity to help them be mindful of experiences that they may not notice easily. These cards can also be useful to keep and use for different activities when you're helping your client become more aware of their private experiences.

Put the "Inside" cards in a sifter or bucket, hand it to your client, and instruct them that they have 60 seconds to sort through as many cards as possible, placing each of them in the right bucket. When the time is up, go through each bucket and count how many correct experiences they sorted. Take the time to purposefully ask your client about what they wrote and why as you go through the sorted cards.

Paying Attention in a New Way — Explore Your World

This worksheet is similar to what we might do in a guided mindfulness exercise where we encourage active participation with in-the-moment feedback from the young people we work with. You might send this worksheet home with your client to fill out.

We also enjoy using this worksheet in session as an exercise by inviting our clients to notice experiences (colors, shapes, textures, smells) that they might not have noticed right away—or taken for granted previously—in the therapy office. You might want to use your office, but we have had a great amount of success (and a lot of fun), leaving the office and walking in through the entrance, into the waiting room, and back into the office for this exercise.

Explore
Your World

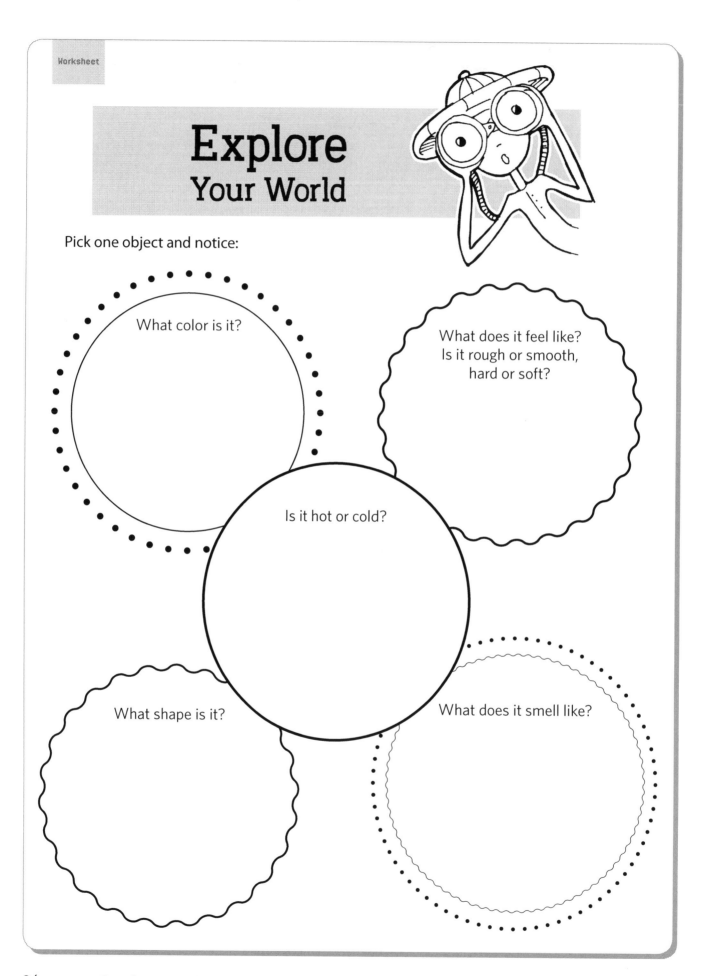

Pick one object and notice:

What color is it?

What does it feel like?
Is it rough or smooth,
hard or soft?

Is it hot or cold?

What shape is it?

What does it smell like?

Listening to the Mind

Teaching young people the skill of distancing themselves from their own evaluations and judgments involves a process by which they can notice the implicit cognitive reactions that may exist.

This exercise is about just that, training a process of being present to the many varied private reactions that can occur across different contexts: pleasant, such as something a young person might enjoy, or unpleasant, such as something that might be aversive.

We're going to give you a handful of examples for this exercise with a wide variety of materials or media that you can use. Similar to Feelings Tic-Tac-Toe, once we introduce this exercise, we return to it over multiple sessions, generally doing it in every session after we introduce it. This exercise quickly becomes a favorite with our young clients.

Instructions

- Pick something for your client to notice.

    ○ Pick something different each time you practice this exercise. You might even repeat this exercise a few times in one session, using different items—our favorite is to mix up the exercise with different types of items: smells, objects, videos, and sounds.

- Guide your client to come in to the present moment, noticing any experiences that might be showing up.

    ○ You may want to guide a brief mindfulness exercise including a yoga practice to settle in, if appropriate.

    ○ Specifically, have your client notice any experiences they may be feeling in the moment. They do not have to identify anything profound or upsetting, simply have them tune into their thoughts, feelings, memories, or physical sensations in this moment.

- Inform your client that you're about to give them something to pay attention to for a little while. You want them to pay extra attention to what their mind has to say about what you show them. If they're comfortable with it, invite them to say the things that they notice out loud.

- Present the item you've chosen to your client for one minute or so.

- After the allotted time, invite your client to first describe the experience, pointing out observations that they noticed—the object's physical properties.

    ○ Observations include descriptions, such as a shape, smell, color, and texture. On the other hand, a judgment or evaluation would be whether they like the experience, think it's good or bad, pleasant or unpleasant, or strange or familiar.

- If they engage in judgments or evaluations, call them out! We like to be playful and say, "Hey, did I just catch you making a judgment!?"

- Allot some time for your client to complete their observing before asking them to describe any judgments, evaluations, or opinions their mind came up with about the experience.

  - You may need to give specific prompts ("What did you think about X?"), returning to the experience they just had and encouraging a more explicit recounting of what was happening in their mind.

- Wrap up the exercise by explaining that minds are always active, producing both observations and judgments. And that your work together seeks to help them notice their judgments and how those judgments can impact what they think and do.

Two Paths

This worksheet focuses on helping your clients increase their moment-to-moment awareness, thereby increasing their ability to consciously choose what behaviors are workable for them rather than living under the rigid governance of negative reinforcement—attempting to escape painful experiences. We want to increase a repertoire of communicating about prior losses and disappointments, as well as hopes, dreams, and goals for the future.

This worksheet honors a strengths-based approach with an aim that resilience is grown in the presence of painful experiences, not the lack of it. We used this worksheet with a 9-year-old girl we worked with, who had painful traumatic memories that had led to severe attachment consequences and the belief that people she loved would reject her. This worksheet helped demonstrate that acceptance could be a legitimate strategy for her to bring these painful experiences into the present, where she could begin to learn about and understand these experiences in a way that could fortify her in the presence of them.

The worksheet depicts a fork in the road with a path going in two different directions. Instruct your client to write down (in any way they choose) or draw what each direction entails.

Pathway to the Past
This can include setbacks, losses, hurts, and disappointments, as well as happy memories, important people, skills, or lessons learned that are useful.

Pathway to the Future
This can include hopes, dreams, goals, and possible outcomes that the young person wants.

What Will You Find
on Each Path?

Pathway
To The
Future

Pathway
To The
Past

The Thought-Generating Machine

Throughout this book, we seek to teach novel approaches to mindfulness that specifically train young people to contact the present moment, notice judgments, and be aware of reactions. If relaxation is a by-product, that's wonderful, but we don't view relaxation or feeling better as the outcome we seek. This playful take on a mindfulness exercise is one we've found very successful when using with children and adolescents. In our experience, we find it easy for the young people we work with to engage in this activity, and its accessibility extends to them understanding *how* to do it. It's simple: You just notice whatever your mind does.

Instructions

- Explain that this exercise is just about paying attention to anything the mind comes up with. You might liken the mind to a machine that generates thoughts continually.

- Offer to go first in this exercise, modeling how to do it for your client. Tell them that after 15 or 20 seconds, you'll stop and they can take over. Once your client agrees, begin.

- Start by parroting anything your mind might be producing. For example, "I'm noticing the color of your shirt and the design on it. I really like it! I'm feeling a bit funny saying this out loud, assuming you think this is an odd activity. Okay, I'm noticing you smiling and that's making me feel a little relaxed, like you get what we're doing here, and I'm thinking to myself that I might not look so odd now. I'm noticing the lights are a little bright and I'm feeling very relaxed now."

- After a little while, pause and prompt your client to take a turn.

- After they have completed their turn, you might do one more round each or end the exercise there.

- Take some time to debrief what their experience of the exercise was and explain that no matter where they are or what they are doing, their mind is coming up with reactions to it. We like to finish our debrief by saying, "Your mind has something to say no matter what is going on. Your job is to notice it."

Take Mindfulness with You

This exercise has delivered more than its fair share of mileage for us, and we hope you find it as beneficial as we have and continue to! We long struggled to make mindfulness practices directly applicable to the lives of the young people we work with.

Mindfulness is a practice. It's something you do and will probably need to repeat many times before you feel like you've mastered it. You don't simply finish being mindful or check it off a list: "Mindfulness, done for today!" Instead, understand that mindfulness is a state of mind that you learn to cultivate in your daily life, and you can return to it over and over throughout the day. One of the early pioneers in bringing mindfulness to Western health practices, Jon Kabat-Zinn (1994), defined mindfulness as paying attention (noticing), on purpose, in the present moment, nonjudgmentally.

Our hope is to present you and your clients with a mindfulness practice that increases their ability to simply notice private experiences (thoughts, feelings, sensations, or memories). Once they have this practice down, they can then use their new mindfulness skills to practice creating a distance between themselves and their painful private experiences through observing thoughts, feelings, sensations, or memories that would trigger them to engage in problematic behaviors.

Even if judgments show up as they practice, our recommendation is that they notice them, too. You may even want to show in the session how easy it is to have judgments about different items. For example, you could hold up different markers, books, or toys and ask them for their opinion. If they are older, ask them if they see anything they cannot judge or affix some evaluation to? We'd wager that they likely can't. We judge everything that we observe. So, our focus is on simply training the practice of noticing.

Take Mindfulness with You

Noticing is the skill we seek to increase, and while some children and adolescents may be more open to practice more seated, traditional forms of mindfulness practice, some may struggle at first to sit still or with their eyes closed. That is why we suggest you provide a handout to them, or their caregivers if they are younger, for them to practice over the week. Instruct them to take a few moments out of their day to try one or more of the following:

- Take a breath on purpose, wherever you are, whatever time it may be. Notice the sensations of your breath in your body, and the rise and fall of your chest and belly.

- When you're riding in the car, turn off any distractions like the radio, song, or podcast you might be listening to. Notice what you see, the quality of the light entering the space you're in, the rumble of the seat underneath your body, sounds you can hear, the temperature of the air on your skin. (Caregivers can prompt this by asking questions such as: "What do you see?" or "What different sounds can you hear?")

- When eating, take a moment to slow down and eat purposefully. What flavors do you notice? Take in the smell and texture of your food. Take your time to eat and just notice what that experience is like. (This can be an activity the whole family does: eating the first bite of any meal mindfully.)

- During your morning routine—brushing your teeth, washing, getting dressed—go slowly and pay attention to your experience. What do you notice as you spread toothpaste on your toothbrush? Pay attention to the sensations as the toothpaste makes contact with your teeth or tongue.

  - For children who are learning some of these hygiene habits, this can be particularly helpful, as they already need to pay extra attention when they are learning a new skill. Adolescents may need reminders to practice as these behaviors have become perfunctory, but they can still benefit from noticing sensations as they brush their teeth or take a shower—they may be surprised by some of the sensations they notice.

These are only a few examples of the many ways clients can practice being present. Others may include when playing with friends, drawing, going for a walk with caregivers, or other activities that young person particularly enjoys or does regularly. Adolescents may put reminders on their phones to remind them to pay attention throughout the day, whereas younger clients might use the Mindful Reminders worksheet (page 125).

Mindful Walking

You may wish to conduct this exercise in your office or, if appropriate, out in the community during an in vivo exposure session. We'd like to encourage you (if appropriate for your practice setting) to get out of a confined space, such as your office or classroom. This exercise is also appropriate to teach to both young clients and their caregivers, as it may be a helpful exercise for the caregiver and client to practice when at home or walking to school or the park.

Instructions

Instruct your young client to do the following:

- Walk around without having a specific place to go or anything to do apart from walking.

- Any time they notice something they see, say it out loud: "I'm seeing a red car."

- When they have a thought, say it out loud: "I'm having the thought that I like that red car."

- If they have any other thoughts, say them out loud, too: "I think that I might look silly doing this."

- If they have any feelings they can identify, say them out loud: "I'm feeling funny."

TRAINING FUNCTIONAL ANALYSIS IN YOUNG PEOPLE

How Behaviors Work

You may have been surprised when reading this book's introduction to learn that many of the acceptance and mindfulness approaches we use for exercises and worksheets are based on behavioral science. We use the following worksheet as an explicit example of training caregivers to pay more attention to what happens before and after their child's behavior, perhaps facilitating a nonconfrontational conversation about how they may be inadvertently reinforcing their child's problematic behavior.

How Behaviors Work

This worksheet will help to identify what is prompting problematic behaviors in your young child and how those are being reinforced.

Situation: Describe when, and where you were.

The Hook: What happens before a problematic behavior?

The Response: What is the problematic behavior? Explicitly define it.

The Outcome: What happens next as an outcome?

Barriers and Benefits of Behavior

Modeling acceptance, mindfulness, and connection to values can be tricky at times with young people. Although this is anecdotal, we find that young people generally look for the *right* answer to a problem or reach for a solution during a difficult time.

We created this worksheet to keep the conversation focused on what is important, what is going to make that difficult, and why it's important. We especially find this relevant in situations where young people attempt to track our reaction as a helping professional to their response, looking for reinforcement for the *right* answer.

For example, once we were working with a 13-year-old transgender adolescent. They expressed a lot of frustration about their classmates noticing their gender presentation—they wanted to look more masculine and this was especially hard to do without the appropriate hormone treatment they were seeking. We validated their frustration and even voiced our own dismay at the discrimination they were suffering.

There were, however, a handful of things they wanted to do socially and at school. We knew there was no arguing with their mind and that arguing might be experienced as invalidating or outright demeaning. We also knew that acceptance would be a hard sell— we don't want to be perceived as being permissive of this abusive behavior, yet we knew judgments would persist and we couldn't rescue this youth from upsetting comments at school. However, we did want to see them live a vital, meaningful life even during this difficult time.

We introduced this worksheet, asking this adolescent to describe three of the specific small steps related to what they wanted to do. Then, for each of those small behaviors that made up a larger pattern of behavior, we asked, "What's going to make that hard for you? And what about this is important to you?" We encouraged this young person to pay attention to their experience and choose how they want to behave, seeing the pain and connecting with their values.

Through this series of questions they learned that even in the midst of a difficult situation, they are in control of how they respond.

Benefits and Barriers of Behavior
How we face our fears to live our values

Behavior I want to do	What makes it hard?	What's important about doing it?

Behavior I want to do	What makes it hard?	What's important about doing it?

Behavior I want to do	What makes it hard?	What's important about doing it?

Behavior I want to do	What makes it hard?	What's important about doing it?

Background Noise

The Background Noise Worksheet takes the concept of background noise and applies it to the thoughts that pop up for our clients and chatter in the background throughout the day. Before filling this worksheet out, we may ask our clients:

"Are you or someone you know one of those people who always has something playing in the background? Perhaps you have music, the radio, a television, or a podcast on in the background while you go about your day. When you visit any retailer, they typically have music on in the background. Have you noticed that, at first, you hear everything loud and clear, and then eventually you stop noticing it—it becomes background noise unless you listen for it specifically? Maybe every once in a while a song you love comes on or the television show you are watching has a loud action part and you tune in again, but eventually the sounds once again fade into the background.

"Our minds are kind of like that: chattering on in the background until every once in a while something jumps out at us and catches our attention. This worksheet will help you identify what thoughts or memories continue to grab your attention so that we can work on letting them fade into the background, too."

This worksheet makes for a helpful transition when clients leave therapy and go home. To model how to do the worksheet, we typically fill out one or two of the noise sources during the session and then ask the client to complete it at home as they notice more difficult stuff showing up in their lives.

Background Noise

What difficult
thoughts pop up?

When do these
show up?

What do you want to
do when they pop up?

_____

_____

_____

_____

_____

_____

What difficult feelings pop up?

When do these show up?

What do you want to do
when they pop up?

What difficult memories pop up?

When do these show up?

What do you want to do
when they pop up?

_____

_____

_____

PRACTICING ACCEPTANCE

The Complete Collection of Your Life

We want to help young people recognize that our mind, like a good storyteller, has a way of telling the story of our life that may overemphasize difficult moments and underemphasize good moments.

With this worksheet, we identify the different moments in our clients' lives—both joyful and difficult—and help them create an image for what the next chapter in their story will be. This helps us take a step back and show the client that they are on a journey and this phase will transition into a new phase that can be anything they choose.

It can also be helpful to see how the client chooses to portray or depict moments in their lives, as it may give insight into how they have viewed different memories or experiences.

The Complete Collection of
_____ 's Life

Complete the title by writing your name in the blank above. Then draw a cover for each important chapter in your life, including the next chapter.

The Beginning

The Best Day

A Difficult Moment

The Next Chapter

The Hardest Thing to Accept

This is a simple fill-in-the-blank worksheet to help you organize how your painful experiences relate to the rest of your life. Sometimes, writing this down on paper can help you become open to the idea of acceptance or trying something new.

The hardest thing to accept in my life is

_____

_____.

This is difficult for me because I sometimes feel

_____

_____.

When these experiences show up, I might think to myself

_____

_____.

If I could make peace with this pain, I would

_____

_____.

And letting go would mean I'd be free to

_____

_____.

Except that feels hard right now because

_____

_____.

Your Inner Bully

In this worksheet, clients learn different ways to relate to their Inner Bully. Each of us has an Inner Bully: the voice that is critical, belittling, and dictates what we can and can't do.

With this worksheet, you will want to explain what is meant by the Inner Bully and describe that the purpose of this activity is to make our Inner Bully explicit so that we can learn to work with it, rather than wasting energy on attempting to fight it off.

Asking clients to draw a picture of what they imagine their Inner Bully looks like, what it says, and how big it is in comparison to themselves is intended to simultaneously be an exposure to the difficult inner content (judgments, criticisms, etc.) and a way to distance themselves from that content, observing it as a separate source of influence, the Inner Bully character.

Your Inner Bully

- How big is it? Is it big and scary, or small and quick?

- What do their eyes look like (angry eyes, multiple eyes always watching you, one giant eye)?

- Does it have wings, claws, scary teeth, or many arms or hands?

- What type of things does your Inner Bully say about you? Draw a speech bubble for your bully.

- How big are you compared to your Inner Bully?

- Is it chasing you, towering over you, do you have it on a leash? Draw where you are in relation to your bully.

Inner Bullies come in all different shapes and sizes. What does your inner bully look like? **Draw your Inner Bully below.**

Giggle Maps

Many of the young people we work with have heard of GPS: a map app that offers turn-by-turn instructions for driving, walking, and public transit. In this exercise, we like to explain that technology offers many conveniences, making our lives easier—yet glitches and technical difficulties persist. We explain that, sometimes, our mind can work just like a helpful GPS app, giving us useful information; while other times, it sends us in the wrong direction.

In this exercise, we're going to have a play on words with our own app *Giggle Maps*, exposing how our mind can sometimes be unhelpful and give us instructions that are unworkable. The aim of this exercise is to have an externalized experience of the mind and to experiment with not following some of the rigid rules the mind can easily make.

Clinician Note

When working with groups, we break participants into small groups of two and give them five to 10 minutes each to do this exercise. In groups, each young person takes a turn playing the role of Giggle Maps, following their partner around and giving them all different kinds of directions, warnings, and instructions.

Instructions

- Explain what this exercise is about: role-playing Giggle Maps, a made-up app that represents our mind, and the directions, warnings, and instructions it gives us. Describe that this exercise is about learning how to pay attention to the things our mind tells us, noticing when they are helpful and not.

- Instruct your young client to be themselves and that you will play the role of Giggle Maps, giving all kinds of directions, warnings, and instructions.

  ○ For example, we might say, "I'm going to be your Giggle Map app! I want you to walk around the room, do different things, and I'm going to get up and follow you. I'm going to give you directions of where to go and not go, warnings about things, and instructions on specific things. It's up to you to listen to me and choose what you do."

  ○ As the Giggle Maps app, you might say the following, "You should look behind this plant. There might be something interesting there. Don't use your left hand. If you use your left hand the plant may fall on you. Be sure not to step on any cracks while you're walking. It will take you seven minutes to walk the perimeter of this room. Watch out! A piano is falling on you. Take nine steps then stop. Now turn around. Turn around again."

- If working individually with a young person, you may wish to swap roles—allowing them to be your Giggle Maps app for a brief time.

Debrief:

- Take time to explicitly debrief what your client experienced during this exercise. Ask them what they noticed and what they thought of Giggle Maps giving them different kinds of directions, warnings, and instructions.

    ○ If a young person reports to you that this activity was uncomfortable or they were distracted, thank them for noticing! We fear that might sound a little unhelpful to you, our reader, who we respect and very much want to benefit from this book. However, we do want to make therapy a positively reinforcing experience where the young people we work with can be celebrated for doing the work of noticing that we ask of them—even if the perceived outcome isn't as ideal as we'd wish.

- After debriefing, discuss that unlike a maps app on a phone that can be easily closed or turned off, our mind is always on. It loves to give more and more directions, warnings, and instructions.

Who Am I?

This art activity is appropriate for young people of all ages. It is intended to help young people experience themselves as more than their pain by encouraging them to depict both what is most painful in their experience, as well as what is important to them—their hopes, dreams, and qualities they most wish to be about.

Materials

- A large roll of oversized paper.

- Art supplies, including colored pencils, markers, glue, glitter, stickers, and varying images printed and cut out (printed or from magazines).

It's best to lay the paper on a flat surface; walls work especially well. You may need to tape the corners of the page down.

Instructions

- Have your client lean against or lay on the paper. Encourage them to have fun, posing themselves in any way that seems right. Then, trace an outline of their silhouette. Alternatively, if you're doing this exercise in a group, participants can split into pairs and create the silhouette outline for one another.

- Describe to your client that before you have them decorate their silhouette, you want them to take a moment to look at their paper outline: "This is going to be a representation of you. In any way that feels right for you, I'd like to invite you to illustrate different aspects of who you are and how you experience yourself."

- Prompt them to begin decorating their silhouette with any materials they choose while asking, "Maybe think about a moment in your life that you're proud of. How might you reproduce that on your silhouette? Where would you put it? How about a moment that brings up a painful memory, guilt, or shame? How would you show that? Where might you feel that in your body? And where on your silhouette would it go?"

- Follow up during the activity with additional instructions: "Also think about who and what is important to you in your life. How can you demonstrate that on your silhouette? And what about the qualities you want to be about?"

Debriefing this exercise can be just as valuable as doing the exercise itself! Invite your client to notice their silhouette, pointing out whatever might show up for them personally: reactions, thoughts, feelings, etc. Whatever the response, be reinforcing, thanking them for noticing or complimenting them specifically on their ability to point out detail or vivid aspects of their experience.

The Mind Is a Pop-Up

This exercise is one we came up with for adolescents; but considering how accessible online media is to children now, this activity has become relevant to younger and younger client populations. In this exercise, we will make explicit some of the things our minds tell us to do—the ways our mind might instruct us to handle situations. We're going to give you a variety of examples you can use. We like varying them so that we have variability in directives and thoughts.

In addition, some clients may have difficulty filling in the blanks at first. This is okay. Remember that paying attention to our mind in this way is not a common practice and may be unconventional to young people who simply take the content of their mind as fact.

Instructions

- Ask your client: "Have you ever been browsing online and experienced a pop-up window? Sometimes, they tell you things such as you can't do something, that there's something wrong with your device, or that you have to do something like fill out a survey or buy something."

- You can pause and wait for an appropriate response, discuss pop-ups briefly, or take out a device and show clients what a pop-up actually looks like. Follow up with: "What do you do when you get a pop-up? Do you listen to it 100% of the time?"

- Again, pause for a response and then carry on the conversation: "I didn't think you'd always believe pop-ups. I don't always believe them or do what they tell me to do. Here's the interesting thing. Our minds are like pop-ups: We have thoughts all the time about things, and our mind will try and tell us what to do and how to do it. Sometimes, this is helpful and we can make use of what our minds say, and other times not so much."

- The following is a fill-in-the-blank example of a pop-up their mind might have. You can have your client fill in the blanks and then have them imagine this pop-up in their mind, just like one that may show up on a computer screen. Or you can talk them through an eyes-closed exercise where you read the pop-up warning and see how their minds fill in the blanks. You can also send them home and have them imagine their thoughts as pop-ups all week long, then report back to you what they looked like at your next session.

WARNING! Whatever you think, don't even try it. You will FAIL.

It looks like you're trying to have a good day. Don't forget that you're _____.

Uh-oh, your dream of _____ will never come true. Sorry.

STOP! Failure to hide right now will cause you to have a panic attack.

These pop-ups can be helpful because they often seem funny or outlandish, just like an infomercial, a salesman pitch, or an over-the-top computer warning. This leads to a different response to those thoughts (laughing, saying this is ridiculous) than they are used to when these thoughts pop into their head.

Debriefing this exercise is important. Don't take for granted the process of paying attention in the moment to the experience that is happening for the young person you're working with. We're both humorous in our approaches and like to laugh about some of the reactions that can come up when working with our minds, but your style might be entirely different. That's okay!

However, don't miss this opportunity to ask your client what they noticed. Leave that as an open-ended question and illicit as much feedback as you can about what their *experience* of the exercise was. Once done with what they noticed, ask what changed (if anything) and how they can use this outside of the session. For instance, you may ask, "What are the chances you're going to notice your pain pop-up like an advertisement on the internet?"

Say It, Don't Believe It

In this exercise, we have adapted a really fun piece of experimental research (McMullen, Barnes-Holmes, Stewart, Luciano, & Cochrane, 2008) to work with young clients to help them distance themselves from the thoughts that can govern their behavior. In this exercise, we have our young clients say a statement out loud that contradicts what they are doing to demonstrate how what we say and think does not always have to be believed.

When working with clients who suffer from minds that create strict rules—especially when working with a diagnosis of obsessive-compulsive disorder (OCD) or clients who have fears and phobias—we use this exercise to demonstrate how they don't have to strictly follow the rules that their minds create. You will notice that as the exercise continues, we use more evocative examples—this is done purposefully to increase flexibility in the presence of fused mental content.

Instructions

Instruct your client to:

- Say out loud, "I can't lift my arm, I can't lift my arm," while slowly raising their arm.

- Think to themselves, "My legs don't work," while shaking their legs. Kick their legs up in the air, saying aloud, "My legs don't work, I can't move them." Then, walk around the room making up a silly walk—the sillier the better: deeply bending their knees while walking, changing the pace of their walk.

- Sit down, then say out loud, "If I stand up now, the roof will collapse," while they stand up.

- Say out loud, "Okay, but if I sit now, the roof will really collapse," while they sit back down.

Make sure to debrief this exercise. Our favorite prompt (typically while laughing) with our clients is to say, "What happened!?" Return specifically to the things they said out loud and prompt them to recall what their reaction was to saying this out loud, how it felt, and what they thought would happen.

Memeing Around with Thoughts

A popular form of social communication is a meme. A meme is often humorous—typically an image or video that is copied and edited from its source. For example, someone may take a seemingly normal, candid snapshot and add a humorous statement or caption to it.

In this exercise, we're going to encourage you to use websites that do not charge you to create a meme with your client. A couple of meme generation websites where you can create memes for free and also see reference memes for inspiration, include:

- Memegenerator.com
- Knowyourmeme.com

A word of caution: You may want to have images selected in advance, or have a meme already prepared for your client, as browsing websites for producing memes can sometimes result in popularly generated memes that are offensive for any variety of reasons.

We suggest taking a popular meme and showing it to your client. You can show them a couple of variations on the popular meme. If they have seen it before, great! If not, that's okay. Once they understand the concept of memes (if they don't already), then explain that you made a meme specifically for them based on the painful content they experience and ask them if they'd like to see it. Remember, most teenagers love sarcasm and this kind of humor, so seeing a meme based on their own experiences will likely evoke laughter. Here are some examples:

A popular meme at the time we wrote this book was a picture of Willy Wonka with a condescending smile. It's commonly referred to as "condescending Wonka" online. We worked with a 16-year-old girl who was struggling with feeling unlovable and had a history of abandonment from important figures in her life. We created a "condescending Wonka" meme that said: "Thinking you're unlovable? Your mind hasn't been wrong before."

Another popular meme is the "Joseph Ducreux/Archaic Rap" meme. It is popular for taking rap lyrics and rewriting them in formal language. Google some; they are really funny. We worked with a 14-year-old girl who struggled with body image issues. We created a "Joseph Ducreux/Archaic Rap" meme that said, "I observe myself in reflective surfaces, and have strong distaste for my appearance."

Both clients thought their personalized meme was hysterical and wanted to show it to all of their friends! It was a great example of taking something that is normally extremely painful and creating a playful, sarcastic relationship with it. They were able to laugh, truly laugh, in the presence of painful content. If they could do that, there's no telling what else they could do the next time their pain shows up.

Voice Changing

The following exercise requires an especially diligent attention to detail. We recommend waiting to do this exercise until you've had some time to develop a strong alliance and working rapport with your client. We give this caveat because this exercise could be experienced as taking serious emotional disturbances lightly or even making light of painful private content if not done within a strong therapeutic alliance and understanding of the exercise's purpose.

The purpose of this exercise is to explicitly acknowledge the painful content that a young person may be suffering with—such as "I'm unlovable" or "I'm broken"—and work to change their relationship to that content. For example, we successfully implemented this exercise with a teen who had a severe sexual trauma history and was suffering with thoughts about how what happened to them would determine what they're capable of. Similar to a car that is damaged beyond repair, they would refer to themselves as "a write-off."

We encouraged them to say aloud the statement their mind had about them: "Because of what happened to me, I can't have a future. I'm a write-off." We showed empathy for how severe that thought was, thanked them very much for participating, and asked on a scale of 0 to 10 how distressing that thought was. They told us it was a 10 out of 10, and we could understand as much. We then asked on a scale of 0 to 10, how believable that thought was and they said it was again a 10 out of 10. That thought was completely believable.

Having already explained the exercise fully, we unlocked a tablet with a voice-changing app preinstalled—these are often free and easy to find regardless of what operating system/device you have. We had this teen say their painful statement aloud again into the app: "Because of what happened to me, I can't have a future. I'm a write-off." The app recorded their statement, and the client could then select a variety of voice synthesizers and filters. The one they first selected was to have Darth Vader (deep voice, scuba diving respirator and all) repeat their words back to them. Their immediate reaction was to smirk. They pressed a different button, having a chipmunk—voice high and squeaky, the pace sped up rapidly—repeating, "Because of what happened to me, I can't have a future. I'm a write-off." They burst out laughing.

We paused in that moment, and asked, "What just happened there?" They responded, "It's just hilarious and ridiculous." We asked how distressing and believable that statement was coming from Darth Vader or from a chipmunk, and they responded, "It's super distressing but way less believable. It's funny because it still hurts, but I'm just like... whatever, it's there."

Instructions

- Search for and download a voice-changing app on your mobile device. Understand how to use it before implementing this exercise into the session.

- Explain the exercise to your client, describing that although we can't get rid of our thoughts, we can experiment with them, hearing them differently. This can help us get some space or "breathing room" when they show up so we can more easily do the things we want to in life.

- Invite your client to identify a painful thought—something difficult their mind tells them—and to say it out loud.

- Encourage them to identify how they experience this statement—how distressing and believable it is.

- As they record, and then listen to, their painful thought in different voices, check in with them to see what they are noticing, and finally ask how distressing and believable the thought is now.

All Bad News, All the Time

Making the painful things a young person's mind says about them explicit can be a useful way to train the present moment, training a sort of anytime, anywhere mindfulness. In this exercise, we introduce an attempt at cognitive distancing from painful material and experiment in a playful way with how a young person relates to their pain.

We create a metaphor for the mind as a helicopter reporter working for a local broadcast called KBBN: the all bad news all the time network. We explain to our young client that we will play the role of their mind, reporting with gusto and enthusiasm about all the "bad" news or shortcomings we can deliver about them. We will also somberly report their successes.

Materials

You don't need materials for this exercise, but we've had some fun being playful with our young clients, including using this exercise in groups with adolescents. When working in groups we use plastic cups, which the person playing the role of the helicopter reporter can talk into, altering their voice to sound compressed like it's originating from a helicopter's headset.

In the previous exercise, we referenced the many voice-changing apps that are available for mobile devices. There are a variety of toys and other novelty products that can be used to alter your voice in real time—we did find one toy that has a setting to alter your voice to make it sound like there's a helicopter in the background while your voice comes through a megaphone. However, these are not a necessity; they simply add to the fun of the exercise. Perhaps we could say that a sense of humor is required for this exercise.

Instructions

- Give some structure to this exercise by explaining that you're going to play the role of a radio host announcing various experiences, but the radio station is KBBN, the all bad news all the time network, which means that you will be commenting on all the negative things a client tells you they are thinking or experiencing.

- Invite your client to share some difficult things with you that they have been struggling with more recently: thoughts, feelings, sensations, memories.

  ○ You can use your prior knowledge of them to inform your work.

- Using the content you have just received from your client, and also integrating some material that you know about, put on your best announcer voice and begin your broadcast.

  ○ For example, we'll use ourselves (Tim and Jessica as example clients with Karsyn, our editor, playing the role of the therapist): "Hello! This is Karsyn, your KBBN afternoon host reporting live at the scene of Tim and Jessica's latest book, *The Acceptance and Mindfulness*—whatever that means—*Toolbox for Children and Adolescents*. I'm excited to share that it is a failure! That's right, everyone who has read it hates it and the reports are pouring in. Tim is indeed not any good at his job and Jessica is definitely an imposter. They've really done it this time, their worst dreams are coming true."

- Pause and ask your client what it's like to hear this broadcast. Do a thorough debrief of what they think of it, whether it's believable or not, and how it impacts what they think about the very real issues they've shared with you.

- Ask for some achievements that the young person you're working with has accomplished. It could be anything big or small—something that you could view as being celebratory.

  ○ Use examples that you've noticed this young person has accomplished in therapy, instances where you might be proud of them for sharing or trying something new.

- Once more, use this celebratory content, announcing it out loud as a broadcast or helicopter reporter; however, this time you'll be reporting this news in a somber tone. Remember it's *good* news and you're supposed to be announcing for *bad* news.

  ○ We'll again use ourselves as an example: "Hello listeners. This is Karsyn reporting live on *The Acceptance and Mindfulness Toolbox for Children and Adolescents* situation. Sadly, we have received news that a positive review of the book was leaked online. Both Jessica and Tim were spotted smiling and celebrating. Obviously this must come as a shock to you as it does to me. We're sure things will normalize again and that these two authors will go back to feeling terrible and making mistakes. But, in the meantime, we will keep you updated. Reporting on this sad day from KBBN, all bad news, all the time."

- Taking the time to debrief once more, ask your client what their experience of the second broadcast was, inquiring about what they noticed and what it was like to have heard their successes announced as if it was bad news.

What Do They See?

We have had a lot of success training perspective taking and empathy with brief exercises such as this one. It can also be a fun excuse to get out of the office or use media to promote perspective-taking abilities with the young people we work with.

Materials
Although you can do this exercise without any materials or media, we recommend using pictures of people, short stories (including picture books), or short YouTube or Vine videos.

Instructions
- Present a situation to your client—whether showing them a photo and describing the situation the person in the photo is in, reading a segment of a short story, or showing a brief video. You may want to begin with more simple or clear examples first and then build up to more difficult or complex examples.

- Encourage your client to specifically describe what this person would have seen or heard, what it might have felt like to be them, and what they might be feeling in that moment.

- If a client is unable to come up with a response, or comes up with an incorrect response, it is appropriate to correct the client and explain the correct answer.

This exercise can be done over multiple sessions as a way to both retest and increase skill building.

Take Your Monster with You

This play on our Who's Your Monster? exercise from the previous chapter encourages the young people we work with to draw their yucky feelings monster again. For continuity, you may want to have a copy of the previous artwork and encourage your client to draw themselves in contrast to their yucky feelings monster.

Instructions

- First, ask your young client to tell you about the varying situations that their yucky feelings monster interferes with in their lives: school, social events, sports, whatever may be important to them. You might even ask, "Where does your mind tell you that you cannot go with your monster? And what happens when your mind tells you that you cannot go out to this place or to see this person with your monster?"

- Then, encourage them to draw a rope or string, tethering themselves to their yucky feelings monster, and invite them to imagine taking their yucky feelings monster for a walk. They can't get rid of them so what might happen if they brought their monster with them?

- Introducing self-compassion, you might challenge this young person to view their yucky feelings monster as having nowhere else to go. You can use different imagery, such as their monster as a puppy who is following them around. Or a new younger sibling who wants to always spend time with them. Or that this young person is home to their monster.

Giving Compassion

For this brief, compassion-focused exercise, we have the young people we work with imagine that an inanimate character (such as a doll or stuffed animal) is in a difficult situation, and then invite our clients to give compassion to them.

Materials
- A stuffed character or a baby doll. Stuffed animals also work.

Instructions
- Place the stuffed character or baby doll near to your client—perhaps on their lap or on a table in front of them. We have had some success in asking clients to name the character and identify characteristics about them, including their likes and dislikes.

- Invite them to look at this inanimate character and to imagine it in a difficult situation, feeling emotional, scared, and upset.

- Prompt your client to imagine what they might be feeling and to interact with them in a kind and gentle way.

- Encourage your client to talk softly to them, pick them up and hold them, rock them from side to side.

- Instruct them to pause and take a breath all the way in and notice what it's like for them to interact with this character.

- Elicit from your client how this inanimate character might be feeling now, having been spoken to softly and held in a gentle way.

- Finish this exercise by having the young person describe to you how they can take care of themselves in this kind and gentle way, just like they have shown to the stuffed character or baby doll.

Adolescents may, understandably, not connect with a baby doll or stuffed animal. For older children, it may be helpful for them to imagine a friend of theirs, rather than a stuffed character or baby doll, to connect with in a kind, gentle, and compassionate way.

My Hidden Pain

When encouraging our clients to practice acceptance, we offer multiple examples of being accepting of and interacting with painful private content that they have struggled with. In this art-based activity, we encourage the young people we work with to create a symbol or phrase representing their painful private content in the form of a temporary tattoo that they can wear in an inconspicuous place if they choose to keep it (hidden under a shirt sleeve, etc.).

We use this activity with our individual clients, and have also had a great deal of success with this activity in groups of teens. During one such group, in working with adolescent, self-harming girls, one participant had disclosed a history of sexual trauma. She created a temporary tattoo representing not the sexual trauma she experienced, but a judgment that troubled her deeply: "I'm disgusting." She depicted the judgment as a toxic symbol with the words "I'm disgusting" integrated into the symbol.

It was simultaneously profound and tragic. She depicted it on a part of her body that she could easily hide under her clothing. When we asked if she wanted to remove the design or keep it, she said she wanted to keep it. When we asked what it would be like to leave the group wearing it, she told us it was important to her because she can't leave it behind anyway, so she might as well take it with her and figure out how to live with it.

Materials
- Eyeliner pencils work the best, especially those that are not liquid or meant to have an oily/shiny finish. Feel free to choose multicolored pencils; the ones that can be sharpened are useful.

- Once finished with the design, your client may opt to apply a light coating of hairspray that can act as a sealant to stop the design from smudging.

Instructions
- Tell your client that in this activity you're going to ask them to depict something they've been struggling with as a design and/or words.

- Explain the concept of a temporary tattoo, that it's nonpermanent and that we design it and wear it in the session to experiment with how we relate to it, to see that it's something we experience and walk around with but that it isn't us—who we are.

- Invite your client to recall something painful that they're struggling with, to imagine it as separate, perhaps external from themselves.

  ○ Allow some time for them to imagine shapes, colors, a symbol, or phrase that they could depict, representing this painful thought, feeling, sensation, or memory.

- Encourage them to choose a spot on their body where they can draw this depiction on their skin.

  ○ Remind your client that the tattoo is temporary. This activity is an experiment where they get to be creative—there's no wrong answers.

- Have the client apply the eyeliner pencil to make a design directly on bare, dry skin that is relatively free from hair. We'd like to encourage you, the therapist, to do one too.

Echoes of Another in Yourself

When we work with groups of young people in this acceptance and mindfulness approach, we notice that group cohesion is very strong and we can typically talk about vulnerable topics with ease. What this also means, though, is that ending our work together can be difficult for a variety of reasons: Ending therapy brings up issues of grief and loss, difficulties in saying goodbye to people they have met in their group, feeling scared that progress will halt once they are no longer in the group, and more. Emphasizing the connection to group members and shared experiences can be a powerful way to show that they are never truly alone.

We find this exercise succinctly demonstrates the overall purpose of the group: Private pain is a shared experience that many can relate to and that ultimately a connection with one's values in the present moment affords freedom to be flexible in responding to pain.

Materials

- Balloons—we once again advise that you take extra precaution regarding sensitivities to latex and investigate alternative balloons if necessary.

- Permanent markers

Instructions

- Invite each young person in your group to blow up a balloon, tie it (you may also have balloons already inflated and tied in preparation), and write something that they have been struggling with in their life.

   - Instruct participants not to write their names on the balloons, but just to write about a painful experience they've been struggling with.

- Once each participant has finished, have them throw their balloons in the air, instructing them not to let the balloons touch the floor.

- After a minute or so of keeping the balloons off the floor, tell participants to stop and hold the balloon closest to them—there should be enough balloons for every participant.

- Have each participant read the balloon they are holding aloud. Instruct participants that if they're holding their own balloon, that's okay—no one will know it's their balloon.

- Debrief this exercise by having each participant share what it was like to write their experience, have it leave their hands, and have it read aloud, as well as what it was like to hear all the other experiences, or to read someone else's experience aloud.

Ending and Generalization

These practices help us plan for maintenance phases, set longer-term intentions to change both with our young clients and with their caregivers, and transition to concluding therapy. Transitions and ending therapy can be a difficult time for children and adolescents, as saying goodbye may be an experience they have little practice with or one that is associated with painful memories.

Our goal is to help clients generalize the skills they learn in therapy to other areas of their lives and set them up for success no matter what they are striving toward or what challenges they meet.

TRAINING SKILLS FOR OUT OF SESSION SUCCESS

Process Heroes

The young people we work with—whether it be children from three years old all the way up to adolescents, and even their caregivers—seem to really like superheroes these days! Referencing superheroes can be a great benefit in the therapy room, as the stories of superheroes demonstrate a combination of strength and struggle, and the application of special abilities—sometimes called superpowers.

We seek to train special abilities in our young clients—acceptance, mindfulness, a connection to values, and compassion—that can be applied to a variety of life situations.

We like to use the six Process Hero cards to describe complex psychological processes in a simple way with the young people we work with: committed to what's important with Captain Commitment; aware of experiences with Vigilance, and so on. Sometimes when working with a young client, we'll pick one card in particular we feel is most relevant to them, that can assist in the difficult situation they face.

Other times, we will present all the cards to the young people we work with and ask them what Process Hero's special ability they might need in order to address an upcoming scenario or a past hurt.

We may also train caregivers in understanding the different Process Heroes so that they can cue their young person to draw on that hero's superpower in a situation outside of the therapy room.

Have fun and be creative with the Process Hero cards. Remember, the aim of this work is to facilitate conversations, examples, and practical next steps with acceptance and mindfulness. These heroes can help you describe the ways of being that lead to more flexible repertoires.

Process Hero Cards

Captain Commitment

Captain Commitment focuses on doing what works no matter the situation he's faced with.

Special Abilities: Does what's important even when it's hard.

Merit

Merit looks for values everywhere and is often called on when situations are difficult.

Special Abilities: Can locate who and what matters anywhere, any time.

Vigilance

Vigilance keeps a close eye on what is happening in every moment. Always watching, always vigilant, always ready!

Special Abilities: Identifies experiences: good, bad, or neutral; Vigilance notices everything.

The Look Out

The Look Out works from a distance, watching and tagging experiences before they get close.

Special Abilities: Can tell experiences apart from people; can see the whole world from the watch point.

The Human Container

The Human Container can adapt to any situation, receiving all experiences regardless of how pleasant or difficult.

Special Abilities: Holds every type of experience: good, bad or, neutral; can expand to contain everything.

Dr. Fusion

Dr. Fusion can make imagination feel like real life and reverse real-life fears and thoughts to imagination.

Special Abilities: Makes imagination believable and makes experiences unbelievable.

Mindful Reminders

Providing reminder cards has been extremely useful for us when helping the young people we work with to stick with long-term behavior change. When working with a young boy who struggled daily with fears and painful reactions to his fears, we implemented mindful reminders as a way to have him pause throughout his day and notice what he was experiencing. The reminders were strategically placed using tape: one at the foot of his bed that he would see every morning when he woke up, another inside his backpack, and another at the back of his cubby hole where his belongings were placed at school—he would see this one at the beginning of his school day, before and after breaks, as well as at the end of his school day.

Upon returning to a future session, he shared, "Every morning when I see my reminder, I wake up really slowly, moving in slow motion like I'm being mindful of *everything* I do." He said he would exaggerate a long yawn and slow stretch. We laughed together and said, "That's such a great example of you showing me how you can slow down and wake up on purpose, even just as you get out of bed!"

Mindful reminders can be index cards with tape on the back, sticky notes, or whatever else you come up with. Adolescents who have cell phones may want to put reminders on their phones; however, we encourage them to still use more visible reminders, such as sticky notes, as it is harder to ignore than a buzzing or chime on their phone.

This worksheet has three mindful reminders on one page and can be cut on the lines to use for three different reminders or one reminder a child may want to place in three different places.

My Mindful Reminder

My Mindful Reminder

My Mindful Reminder

My Decision Guide

The young people we work with can struggle with acceptance and mindfulness-based interventions, because they assume that there is simply an objective "right" or "wrong" answer to "fix" the problem or concern. Although we agree that there are certainly situations in life with easy answers, these don't tend to be the situations our clients struggle with. We frequently joke with clients: "If this situation was simple and all you needed was a solution, don't you think you would have thought of the answer already? Or, if I was able to solve it quickly, you'd react like: WOW, of course! There's a good chance this isn't that kind of situation, right?"

A 15-year-old we were working with who had some impulse-control issues and was abusing substances wanted to be told how to simply handle each situation. As if we had a fix for his reactivity and could stop substances from medicating him in the short term. He really resisted our discussions and exercises we practiced in session, insisting that it was too hard to slow down and connect with his values when the proverbial poop hit the fan. So we came up with this worksheet. At the time, it was a whiteboard doodle that we did in session. He took a picture of it with his phone and told us he referenced it frequently.

We believe this made a difference with him (and have since used it with many other adolescents as well) because we didn't get into a back and forth argument over whether or not the substances worked in the moment to make him feel better. Instead, we focused on whether or not what he did was helpful to him in the life he wanted to live. That became our criteria going forward: not what we or other people in his life thought was right, but for him to take the time to carefully look at who he wanted to be and how his behavior worked to get him there.

My Decision Guide

This worksheet will help you look at different behaviors you want to do, and see whether those behaviors help you in the long term.

I'm struggling with a painful situation and what I want to do:

Is it helpful for me to do?

YES ↓   NO → What would be helpful for me to do?

Will it help someone else?

YES ↓   NO → What would help someone else?

Is it helpful for the world?

YES ↓   NO → What would help the world?

I care about the situation because:

_____

Do It!

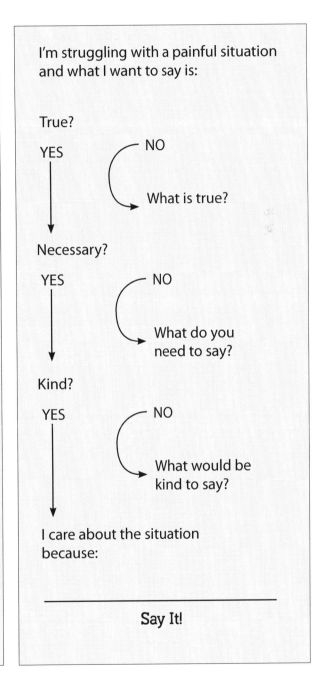

I'm struggling with a painful situation and what I want to say is:

True?

YES ↓   NO → What is true?

Necessary?

YES ↓   NO → What do you need to say?

Kind?

YES ↓   NO → What would be kind to say?

I care about the situation because:

_____

Say It!

127

My Gratitude Journal

This worksheet offers a daily practice for young people to journal about what they appreciate. Gratitude is the quality of being thankful. This gratitude journal allows your clients to show appreciation for what matters to them in their life—no matter how small—and to return some kindness by recognizing its importance.

Gratitude
Journal

Write down one thing you are grateful for every day.

Day 1:

Day 2:

Day 3:

Day 4:

Day 5:

Day 6:

Day 7:

Purposeful Steps

This worksheet, adapted from *The ACT Approach* (2017), draws on SMART goals to help a young client create a detailed plan for building habits or beginning a behavior, while also adding in a values component and identifying potential roadblocks along the way so that they can prepare for any bumps along the road.

Purposeful
Steps

What is important to me about this goal?

Specific

What is the first step you could
take toward your goal?

Tracking

How will you keep track of this goal?
Will you use mindful reminders?
Or check it off when you are successful?

End Date

I will reach my goal by:

Possible

Do you have all the skills and
resources to complete the goal?
If not, how can you get them?
Who can help?

Setbacks

What will make this goal hard? How will I overcome setbacks?

Branching Out

This worksheet shows a tree with roots. The roots represent values, the trunk represents the person who is living, and the branches represent different behaviors they want to do. This helps a client look at their path in life from most abstract (values) to most specific (goals). They can hang this on their wall to represent different steps toward their goal.

Branching Out

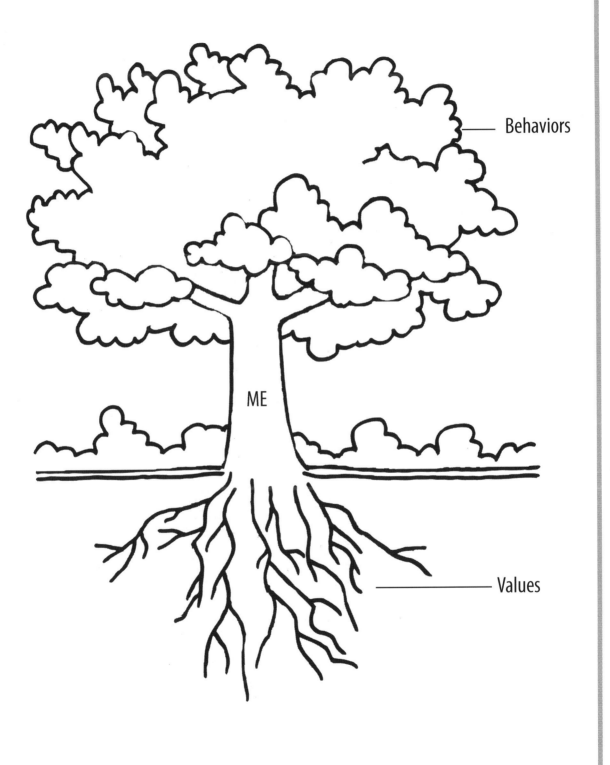

Behaviors

ME

Values

WORKING WITH CAREGIVERS AND FAMILIES

Water Your Flowers

Encouraging caregivers to practice acceptance and mindfulness can be difficult—it doesn't seem like an immediately effective parenting strategy. We often dread the sarcastic and frustrated parent's response: "Oh, accept my kid's bad behavior...of course! Why didn't I think of that?"

Acceptance and mindfulness is a hard sell, especially when caregivers want things better *now*. We understand the push for immediate change, and as a result, it is often our job to explain how reinforcement works—that behaviors persist because they're being reinforced. Neither we nor caregivers may know what is immediately reinforcing about these problematic behaviors for the young people in their lives. So rather than trying to get better at punishment (this is an early priming to later introduce more explicit principles of positive parenting), we aim to reinforce and shape the behaviors we want to see grow.

The following worksheet is what we use to focus a caregiver's attention to this new mindset and directly apply our favorite metaphor in working with caregivers: Your relationship with your children is a garden, and your attention is the watering can. Water what you want to see grow. Don't water the weeds.

Water Your
Flowers

Only things we water and nurture will grow. What behaviors do you want to grow in your young person? Write them on the flower petals. Write problematic behaviors on the lines that represent weeds.

STOP and ACE IT

This Stop and ACE IT worksheet encourages caregivers to pay closer attention to the function of behaviors for themselves and the young people in their lives. It also promotes empathic communication through asking questions, rather than giving directions or challenging.

When faced with a painful situation: Stop and ACE It!

Acceptance: What is showing up inside of me as a caregiver that makes this situation difficult? What feelings am I having? What thoughts or judgments do I have right now? What does this remind me of?

Curiosity: What is showing up inside of my child? What might they be thinking? How are they feeling right now? What is it like to be them?

Empathy: Ask how they feel or help them label it (i.e., "You look really upset with me right now."). Show them that you're curious about how they feel (i.e., "Wow, I had no idea you were angry about this.").

IT!

Family Tattoo

When working with a young person and their caregiver, we have an intimate exercise that we have had a great amount of success with. For the families you work with, the term *tattoo* may not be appropriate so you can, of course, modify and adapt this exercise. Instead of using the word *tattoo*, you could call it a family crest or an emblem.

Throughout therapy with families, we cover a lot of different topics: We focus on difficult experiences, often labeling them and discussing them explicitly with an aim to be mindful, but we also practice acceptance when difficult content shows up. We also take time to purposefully author values, focusing on who the young people we work with want to be; and in the long term, distill reinforcers for the caregivers we work with. It would be out of place for us to begin wrapping up therapy by telling our clients what they should do or who they should be, so instead we invite the young people and caregivers to participate in this exercise together.

Materials

- We recommend using washable markers, and have had the most success with paintbrushes that have washable ink internally.

- Having flexible stencils handy is ideal but not necessary.

Instructions
We ask each caregiver and young person we've been working with to make a tattoo for one another based on our work together and their hope for the future. The tattoo can be a symbol that is meaningful, words, or a combination of symbols with words. They can create this tattoo directly on the other person, or the young person and caregiver can draw this tattoo on a piece of paper.

Encouraging Positive Parenting

A phrase we say to caregivers so often that we worry they think it's our personal mantra is, "Catch your kids being good." It's somewhat antithetical to the caregivers we work with to think about focusing on positive reinforcement rather than punishment. We explain that, sometimes, caregivers can inadvertently reinforce problematic behaviors by paying attention to them; and, at times, even punishing the behavior can be reinforcing because the caregiver may be giving the child attention that child would not receive if they were behaving well. Therefore, our intervention is to have caregivers focus on reinforcing the behaviors they want to see persist in their children (or behaviors they generally want to see more of).

With this Good Behavior Tracker, we begin by asking caregivers to list behaviors the young people in their life are already doing that they want to continue, and to add a few target behaviors that will likely require special attention to reinforce and become consistent. If we're given feedback that a young person performs zero reinforceable behaviors, then that's no problem; just target even small improvements in behavior with the tracker.

Tracking good behavior begins by first identifying specific behaviors for a young person to perform. Second, you reinforce the behavior by acknowledging it: verbal praise with "good job" or a pat on the back works. Keeping the good behavior tracker in a visible spot, such as on the fridge, is a good idea. Next, place a check or smiley face on the day the behavior was performed. We encourage caregivers to use a cumulation of points over the course of a day to earn a young person something: tablet or gaming time, etc. This monetization of things/activities that a young person can take for granted in their home life is essential.

Our aim isn't to be cold or distant; instead, we look to praise and give opportunities for the young people we work with to earn what they value. For example, getting up without multiple prompts, brushing teeth, and bringing home school work might each receive a check for good behavior. Two checks can be cashed in for 30 minutes of tablet time. Find other examples of what is reinforcing for the young person and encourage the caregivers you work with to evaluate how many checks they're worth.

The Good Behavior Tracker has a daily total. We recommend adding these up at the end of the day for a daily reward that is based on how many behaviors were accomplished, and adding up the daily totals for the week (regardless of how many checks have been cashed in) for a larger reward. A low-level reward might be choosing what the family has for dinner on Saturday. A higher-level reward might be going to the movies or some other valued activity. Remember, the purpose of using good behavior tracking is to reinforce the right behaviors.

Good Behavior Tracker

Name: _____

Week: _____

Good Behaviors	S	M	T	W	T	F	S	Total
Daily Totals:								

What I've Learned

Young people can have a difficult time saying goodbye. This worksheet is a helpful way to begin the goodbye process, inviting your young client to reflect on their experience with you: remembering what it was like to attend therapy, what they've learned about therapy, and more details to consolidate the work they've done.

Please feel free to adapt this worksheet, add to it, or remove what doesn't feel useful. One of our favorite adaptations of this worksheet is to have it printed on a whiteboard in our office with room for words and pictures.

When I first came to therapy, I thought therapy would be _____

_____.

Now that we're at the end, I can say therapy is definitely about _____

_____.

What I was most hoping to get out of therapy is _____

_____.

And looking back, I'm glad that I _____

_____.

Something I can now do is _____

_____.

Something important for me to remember is that _____

_____.

I hope that in the future I'll be able to _____

_____.

What's important to me about that is _____

_____.

Something I can do to help me stay true to my values is _____

_____.

Preparing for Setbacks

As helping professionals, we know that setbacks are inevitable. Things go wrong, whether it be a family member who suffers with a serious illness or death, a friend who lets us down, a painful interpersonal situation at school, or a big change.

We use this worksheet to be explicit about potential problems and highlight what skills the young person can use when those problems arise.

Preparing for Setbacks
Moving forward means some road bumps along the way

As you take all of the skills you learned in therapy out into the world, you will find yourself facing some bumps along the way. Part of progress is knowing how to get back up when you hit a setback. This worksheet will help you look to the future and identify what difficulties may arise (both inside you and out in the world) and what skills you've learned in therapy to use.

What difficulties may show up in the future with people, school, or other areas of your life?

What skills can I use to overcome setbacks due to private experiences (thoughts, feelings, memories, sensations)?

What skills can I use to overcome setbacks due to difficult situations I may face?

What difficult thoughts, feelings, memories, or physical sensations might show up in the future?

Acceptance and Mindfulness Improvisation

We use this worksheet in both groups and individual treatment. If using it in groups, we recommend using it with adolescents, as the reading and lack of structure can be difficult for children.

In group settings, we break adolescents into pairs and hand them this worksheet to interview one another, doing ACT improvisation on an issue they're experiencing. In individual treatment, we find this worksheet helpful when a young client does not want to talk about the specific content of something they're struggling with—perhaps it's especially traumatic and telling the story is retraumatizing.

We have also had success using this worksheet with young people who are treatment resistant. We show them the worksheet, placing it between us, and tell them we will randomly choose only the questions on the page for them to answer and just see where the exercise takes us—just like in improvisation.

We've received a lot of positive feedback based on the improvisation metaphor. We attempt to make therapy an environment of flexibility and positive reinforcement.

Acceptance & Mindfulness
Improv

> Ask your partner the questions below based on
> an experience they are struggling with.

When those private experiences show up, what do you do to try to avoid, control or escape them? If you were noticing those painful experiences, what would I see you do next?

What behaviors would you like to do that would connect you to people or things that are important to you? What behaviors are you already doing that connect you to who and what matters to you?

Me Noticing

← ──────────────────────────── →

What private experiences (thoughts, feelings, memories, or physical sensations) show up that get in the way of connecting with the people, things and qualities that are most important to you?

Who and what matter to you in your life? What qualities or characteristics do you want to be about?

What does it feel like to do things that connect you with who and what matters most to you? What does it feel like to try to escape, control, or avoid painful private experiences? Which side do you spend the majority of your life living on?

Staying on Track

When therapy ends, clients can have a tendency to revert to old behaviors if they don't have a clear structure for what helps them move forward and stay on track. With this worksheet, we seek to consolidate all the exercises, worksheets, and new behaviors that have worked for our client before terminating, so when setbacks happen (and they will), they have one handy sheet to help them get back on track and do what works.

This was particularly useful with a 12-year-old boy we worked with who we were concerned might fall back on old patterns once they were no longer reinforced by us in session. We spent the majority of a session focused on developing answers to each quadrant, especially talking about "sunny moments" that he experienced out of session (i.e., spending time with friends, going outside, eating dinner with his parents) and relating them to his "values" to do our best to make these behaviors stick!

We also spent a lot of time talking about what we had learned in therapy and writing it down in clear language he understood—drawing on metaphors we had used in session—and identifying concrete behaviors, such as practicing mindful breathing every morning, that had helped him throughout therapy. We talked about how, when he found himself struggling, he could look at this worksheet and begin to start doing these activities and habits to get back on track.

Anecdotally, what we find happens over the long term through follow-up maintenance sessions is that we're not very good at predicting what will be the most meaningful exercises, activities, metaphors, and worksheets for each client. However, we have found that the things they do out of session that assist them in connecting with their values almost always stick if they are clearly identified.

The more we can help them identify what those behaviors and patterns are, the more likely they will be able to notice the connection between those actions, their values, and the impact it's having on their life, and the longer these behaviors will continue.

Staying on
Track

This worksheet will help you identify all the behaviors, exercises, activities, and practices that help you be your best self. Refer back to this worksheet when you have gotten off track.

Mindfulness Practices: Write down all the ways you have learned to pay attention to your experience.

Habits: What are the new habits you have created as a result of therapy that help you be your best self?

Sunny moments: What are all the activities or hobbies you do that help you feel great?

Values: Who and what matter most to you that you want to focus on? What kind of person do you want to be?

Saying Goodbye

We recommend writing down the outcome of this activity so that your young client can have a record of you saying goodbye and can take it home with them and reflect on it personally. We'd also like to encourage your creativity. We have turned this into a short poem-like paper for clients, and we have seen therapists make a certificate of completion for the young client they work with. How can you make the memory of this conversation special?

Instructions

- Tell your client something that you learned or something that has changed for you in your practice since meeting with them. What you share could be as inconsequential as an activity you did together that was fun or engaging, explaining that you're more likely to do an exercise or use a metaphor you innovated *together*. Ask your client to share what they have learned or can do differently in their world based on your work together. Encourage them to be specific, giving examples of exactly what they can do now, outside of the therapy room.

- Next, share what you have most appreciated about working with the young person you're saying goodbye to. This could be something that they demonstrated in therapy, perhaps an example where they courageously shared themselves with you, or a pattern of behavior you saw change or increase over time. Invite your client to share what they have appreciated about their time in therapy working with you.

- Finally, share what you hope for in the future for your client. Don't hesitate to be specific. If you bumped into them five years from now, what would you like to hear them say to you, or what would you want to see them doing? Ask them what they hope for themselves, encouraging them to be specific about what their life would be like, what they would be doing, how they would be living.

References

For your convenience, purchasers can download and print worksheets and handouts from www.pesi.com/ACTKIDS

Borushok, J. (2018). *Master guide to stress: How to survive in a world full of chaos.* Ontario: Your Psychology.

Dixon, M. R. (2015). PEAK Relational Training System: Equivalence. USA: Shawnee Scientific Press.

Gordon, T. (2013). Theorizing yoga as a mindfulness skill. *Procedia Social and Behavioral Sciences, 84,* 1224–1227.

Gordon, T., & Borushok, J. (2017). *The ACT approach.* Eau Claire, WI: PESI Publishing & Media.

Hayes, S. C., Strosahl, K. D., & Wilson, K. G. (2011). *Acceptance and commitment therapy: The process and practice of mindful change.* New York: Guilford Press.

Kabat-Zinn, J. (1994). *Wherever you go, there you are: Mindfulness meditation in everyday life.* New York: Hyperion.

McHugh, L., Bobarnac, A., & Reed, P. (2011). Brief report: Teaching situation-based emotions to children with autistic spectrum disorder. *Journal of Autism and Developmental Disorders, 41*(10), 1423–1428.

McMullen, J., Barnes-Holmes, D., Barnes-Holmes, Y., Stewart, I., Luciano, M. C., & Cochrane, A. (2008). Acceptance versus distraction: Brief instructions, metaphors and exercises in increasing tolerance for self-delivered electric shocks. *Behaviour Research & Therapy, 46*(1), 122–129.